KAFFE'S CLASSICS

For Demitri Metros, Robert Buys and Charles Heim who helped and influenced me from the start. They are sorely missed.

KAFFE'S CLASSICS

25 Favorite Knitting Patterns for Sweaters, Jackets, Vests, and More

KAFFE FASSETT

First American Edition

ISBN 0–316–27503–4
Library of Congress Catalog Card Number 93–78857

10 9 8 7 6 5 4 3 2 1

Published simultaneously in Canada by Little, Brown & Company
(Canada) Limited

Printed in Italy

CONTENTS

INTRODUCTION

Over the past eight years since *Glorious Knitting* was published I've produced many new patterns for knitters to tackle. Half of this output never appeared in my five hardback books. These patterns were instead published in Rowan Collections (some of which are now out of print) or produced as magazine offers. I felt it was time to gather the best of them together in one volume, update the yarns and in some cases give new colourways.

One exception is the Big Diamond jacket (page 9), a design that was in my first book. I include it here partly because no specific yarns were given for it then, and partly as it has proved such a favourite with knitters. I have encountered personal interpretations of it all over the world: I have seen every conceivable colourway and even a few shape adjustments, although most people seem to like its large drapey framework. The sample shown in this book was executed by a loose knitter. Needless to say, it will come out more contained if done in the correct tension.

Knitting still remains my most stimulating yet relaxing activity and I thank the powers that be that I can make a living at it. Knitting is positively designed to take the tedium out of long trips and waiting times – I often nearly miss stops on the train as I'm so totally absorbed in a knitting project. When you are involved in a multi-coloured design, plan ahead and take small amounts of whatever colours you might need to get you through. I always pack my knitting or needlepoint project first when travelling.

Since most of my ideas come from the timeless world of ethnic decorative arts, it's good to see that, some years on, these patterns seem as fresh as ever and a joy to reknit. Classic structures such as tumbling blocks, zigzags and interlocking crosses will never date and should become part of your design vocabulary – I love to see inventive knitters mix them all up. Think of the patchwork blankets you could do with all your tension squares, or by just getting a group of knitters to contribute their colouring of the patterns in this book. It's a great way to experiment with new colour combinations. Simply crochet around each sample piece until they fit together to make

Above *A variation of interlocking crosses forms part of this courtesan's kimono in an old Japanese painting. Why not try knitting this double-outlined version? My single-outlined version, Icon, appears on page 127.*

Below *The whirling star pattern on page 44 in tile form at the Alhambra in Granada, Spain.*

a richly detailed blanket – sell it for charity!

It's wondrous indeed to think how these patterns were born out of man's first attempts at communicating a sense of aesthetic, and how culture after culture has made use of these basic structures to enliven surfaces of boxes, bags, buildings and garments. Interlocking crosses draw upon the Byzantine and Japanese cultures; the tumbling blocks design is found in tile work, parquet floors and patchwork quilts and proves such a natural for knitted garments. In this book I give you my first knitted bedcover design featuring this bold pattern.

Colour is, of course, the most important part of this collection. Many knitters, unused to dealing with intricate palettes, knit one or two patterns by the book and then feel free to play with their own colour combinations. Other less adventurous knitters may feel more hesitant so I have devised tempting recipes to get them moving. So often, knitters who have broken the ice by following a pattern will start to use that same structure to do a flight of their own fantasy.

Left *Tumbling blocks patterns, like this classic old patchwork from the Victoria & Albert Museum, inspired my bedcover on page 63.*

Below *'Honeysuckle and Sweet Peas' by Winifred Nicholson was one of my inspirations for the colouring of the Brocade crewneck on page 69.*

Above *What an inspired use of a simple trapezoid – this old kilim led directly to the Baclava jacket on page 26.*

Right *An ancient mosaic in Ravenna, which inspired my Mosaic design on page 74.*

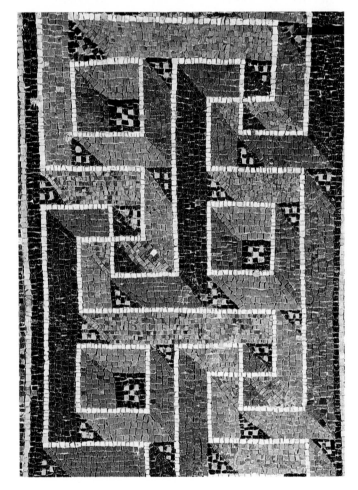

In our workshops we give knitters a painting to match colours from – a Van Gogh or a Matisse provide the colouring for a diagonal stripe or the Big Diamond pattern. There has never been anyone in our workshops who hasn't come up with exciting colour combinations when encouraged to use enough tones in their designs.

Searching for patterns that are good vehicles for colour gives travelling a strong focus: to see how the same patterns were being employed in Asia and ancient Mexico, for example, is fascinating. The ideas in this book span so many cultures and times that I lose count. We have the freedom and luxury of picking the most exciting patterns from the world and from history (sources of inspiration can be found in museums, books, television and magazines). Having these basics graphed out for you gives you the opportunity to try endless variations on the world's great classic patterns.

Many of the designs in this book would make lively scarves as well as sweaters and jackets – just knit a long, repeating band of pattern, or two good-sized pieces for borders around a striped or plain central area. Best of all, knit a sampler scarf of all the pattern structures in the book in a riot of colours or in a tasteful selection of dark, flattering tones. Here's to many happy hours with my favourite occupation!

BIG DIAMOND

I was commissioned by a very generous lady in every sense to design her a flattering jacket. Looking at the task before me I thought of these large pointed diamonds to carry the eye up and down the figure. It was one of the first designs I put in *Glorious Knitting*, without giving any colour or yarn details. I simply knitted one version in bronzy greys and another in pinks and turquoise tones. As I travel about the UK, looking for locations to photograph my finished work, the most consistent colourings I find are multi-shades of greens – hence my choice of lively greens as a basis for this Rowan yarn version of the Big Diamond. I contrast those lovely greens with dark lavenders and rusty golds which make it tone with autumn and spring, summer and even the mossy stones and tree barks of winter. This particular version was knitted by one of my knitters who was in a loose mood and it has come out a lusciously huge size. I've now seen it in millions of different colours all over the world and I look forward to even more!

SIZE AND MEASUREMENTS

One size to fit up to 122cm (48in) bust/chest
Finished measurement at underarm 184cm (74in)
Length from shoulder 75cm (29¾in)
Sleeve length 35cm (14in)

YARN

Rowan Lightweight DK – 25g (1oz) hanks, Magpie – 100g (3½oz) hanks, Lambswool Tweed – 50g (1¾oz) balls, Kid Silk – 25g (1oz) balls, and Donegal Lambswool Tweed – 25g (1 oz) hanks

			Shade no	Amount*
A	Ltwt DK		65	2 hanks
B	Ltwt DK		404	2 hanks
C	Ltwt DK		134	3 hanks
D	Ltwt DK		407	2 hanks
E	Ltwt DK		76	1 hank
F	Ltwt DK		75	1 hank
G	Ltwt DK		106	3 hanks
H	Ltwt DK		36	3 hanks
J	Ltwt DK		73	2 hanks
K	Magpie	Woodland	300	1 hank
L	Lbs Twd	Bluster	184	1 ball
M	Ltwt DK		99	2 hanks
N	Kid Silk	Old Gold	989	2 balls
O	Kid Silk	Pot Pourri	996	2 balls
P	Kid Silk	Steel Blue	991	2 balls
R	Kid Silk	Violet Haze	982	2 balls
S	Don Twd	Leaf	481	2 hanks
T	Ltwt DK		38	2 hanks
U	Don Twd	Juniper	482	2 hanks
V	Don Twd	Roseberry	480	2 hanks
W	Don Twd	Marram	472	2 hanks
X	Don Twd	Cinnamon	479	2 hanks
Z	Kid Silk	Garnet	992	2 balls

Note: The yarns are used in combination, e.g. LL means use 2 strands of yarn L, AL means use one strand of yarn A and one strand of yard L, UUU means used 3 strands of yarn U.
Yarns are shown on the chart by their relevant letters.
*Yarn amounts have been estimated less generously for this jacket, so that the knitter will have as little leftover yarn as possible. Extra yarn can be purchased later, if required, as matching dyelots is unnecessary.

NEEDLES AND BUTTONS

Pair of 4½mm (UK no 7) (US 7) needles
Pair of 5½mm (UK no 5) (US 9) needles
Pair of 6½mm (UK no 3) (US 10½) needles
Circular needle 6½mm (UK no 3) (US 10½) 100cm (40in) long
Seven buttons (optional)

TENSION/GAUGE

13 sts and 19 rows to 10cm (4in) measured over patterned st st using 6½mm (US 10½) needles. *Check your tension (gauge) carefully before beginning and change needle size if necessary.*

NOTES

When working the colourwork pattern, use the intarsia method, using a separate length of yarn for each area of contrasting colour and linking one colour to the next by twisting them around each other where they meet on WS to avoid holes. Read chart from right to left for K (RS odd-numbered) rows and from left to right for P (WS even-numbered) rows unless otherwise stated.

BACK, FRONTS AND SLEEVES (one piece)

Beg at lower edge of back, cast on 90 sts, using 5½mm (US 9) needles and yarns KU.
Work 15 rows in K1, P1 rib in the foll colour sequence:
One row KU, 3 rows BOT, 2 rows HHT, 4 rows AORU, 2 rows FHR, one row BHH, one row BBN and one row CM.
Next row (inc) (WS) Using yarns CM, rib 2, pick up horizontal loop before next st and work into back of it — called *make one* or *M1* —, (rib 3, M1) 29 times, rib 1. (120 sts)
Change to 6½mm (US 10½) and cont in patt from chart (see Notes) for back which is worked entirely in st st, beg with a K row.

Overleaf I chose lively green tones as a basis for this version of the Big Diamond jacket.

9

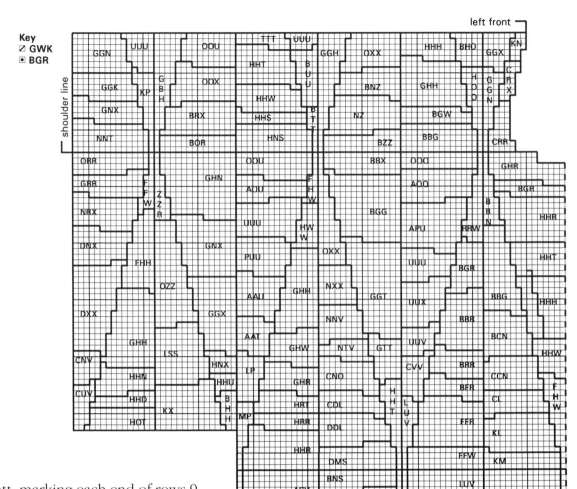

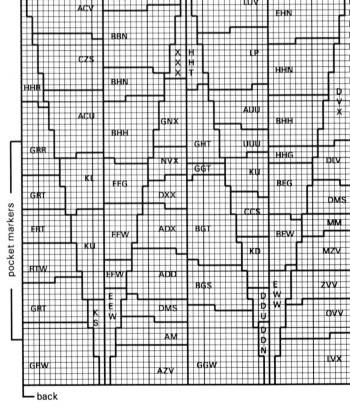

Work 76 rows in patt, marking each end of rows 9 and 43 for pocket openings, so ending with a WS row.

Shape sleeves

Chart row 77 (RS) Using yarn HWW, cast on 30 sts for sleeve, work in patt across these sts, then work in patt across rem sts, with a separate length of yarn BHH cast on 30 sts onto LH needle, then work in patt across these sts. (180 sts)

Change to 6½mm (US 10½) circular needle to accommodate the increased number of sts, then work back and forth in rows as follows.

Cont in patt until chart row 124 has been completed, so ending with a WS row.

Divide for fronts

Chart row 125 (RS) Work 85 sts in patt, then turn and leave rem sts on a spare needle.

Work each front separately, foll chart throughout. Change back to same size ordinary needles at this stage, if desired.

Shape right back neck

Cast (bind) off 4 sts at beg of next row. (81 sts)

Mark each end of last row (chart row 126) for shoulder line.

Work one row without shaping.

Dec one st at beg (neck edge) of next row. (80 sts)

Work without shaping until chart row 135 has been completed, so ending with a RS row.

Shape front neck

Inc one st at beg (neck edge) of next row and every foll 4th row 6 times in all (86 sts), then

work 3 rows without shaping and cast on 4 sts at beg of next row (90 sts), and AT THE SAME TIME when chart row 147 has been completed turn chart upside down and beg at chart row 105 with a P row, cont in patt as set, foll chart back towards row 1.

Work without shaping until front sleeve matches

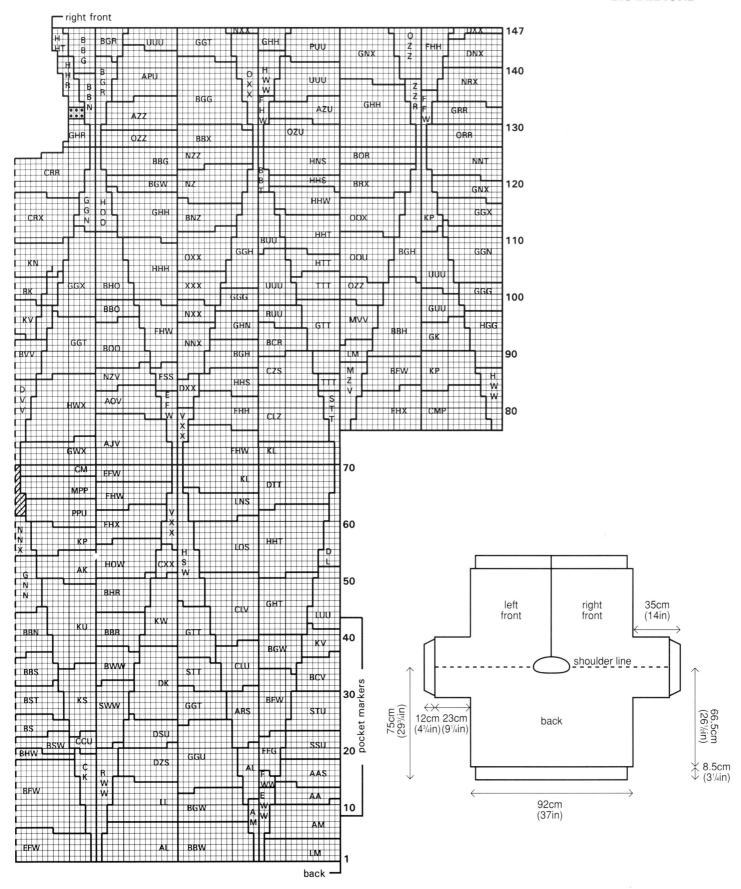

— right front

back

left front | right front | 35cm (14in)

shoulder line

12cm (4¾in) | 23cm (9¼in)

75cm (29¼in)

66.5cm (26½in)

8.5cm (3¼in)

back

92cm (37in)

pocket markers

back sleeve from shoulder line (100 rows in all on sleeve), ending at cuff edge.

Shape sleeve
Cast (bind) off 30 sts at beg of next row. (60 sts)
Work without shaping until chart row 1 has been completed, marking position of pocket opening on side edge as for back, so ending with a WS row.

Change to 5½mm (US 9) needles and work dec row as foll:
Next row (dec) (RS) Using yarns CM, *K2, K2tog, rep from * to end. (45 sts)
Work 14 rows in K1, P1 rib, reversing colour sequence given for back.
Cast (bind) off evenly in rib, using yarns KU.

With RS facing, rejoin yarn to rem sts, cast (bind) off centre 10 sts, work in patt to end. (85 sts) Complete left front to match right front, reversing all shaping.

POCKET EDGINGS (both alike)

Press piece gently on WS, using a warm iron over a damp cloth and avoiding ribbing.
With RS facing, using 5½mm (US 9) needles and yarns KU, pick up and K26 sts evenly between pocket markers on side edge of front.
K one row (WS) to form foldline.
Work 4 rows in st st, beg with a K row.
Cast (bind) off loosely and evenly.

POCKET LININGS

With RS facing, using 6½mm (US 10½) needles and yarns KU, pick up and K26 sts evenly between pocket markers on left side edge of back and work in st st, beg with a P row, and AT THE SAME TIME cast on 4 sts at beg of first row and dec one st at beg of next row and every foll K row until 17 sts rem.
Cast (bind) off evenly.
Work right pocket lining as given for left pocket lining, reversing all shaping.

CUFFS (both alike)

With RS facing, using 5½mm (US 9) needles and yarns SUU, pick up and K78 sts evenly across sleeve end.
Work 5 rows in st st, beg with a P row, in the foll colour sequence:
2 rows SUU, 2 rows PUU and one row of BBT.
Next row Using yarns BBT, (K2tog) to end. (39 sts)
Work 4 rows more in st st, beg with a P row, in the foll colour sequence:
One row K, 2 rows VVX and one row CM.
Next row Using yarns CM, *P3, P2tog, rep from * to last 4 sts, P4. (32 sts)
Work 15 rows in K1, P1 rib, reversing colour sequence given for back.
Cast (bind) off loosely in rib, using yarns KU.

BUTTON BAND

With RS facing, using 5½mm (US 9) needles and yarns BB, pick up and K90 sts evenly along left front edge for woman's jacket or right front edge for man's (12 sts along ribbing, and 78 sts along main part), leaving shaped neck edge unworked.
Change to yarns SUU and P one row.
K 2 rows to form foldline.
Change to 4½mm (US 7) needles and work 8 rows in st st, beg with a K row.
Cast (bind) off loosely and evenly.

BUTTONHOLE BAND

With RS facing, using 5½mm (US 9) needles and yarns BB, pick up and K90 sts as for button band along other front, and AT THE SAME TIME make buttonholes while picking up sts as foll:
Pick up and buttonhole row (RS) Pick up and K2 sts, *pick up and K2 sts, lift 2nd st on RH needle over first st and off needle, pick up and K one st, lift 2nd st on RH needle over first st and off needle, pick up and K11 sts,* rep from * to * 6 times more, but ending last rep pick up and K one st instead of 11.
Next row Change to yarns SUU and purl across row, casting on 2 sts to replace those cast (bound) off on previous row.
K 2 rows to form foldline.
Change to 4½mm (US 7) needles.
Next row (buttonhole) K2, *cast (bind) off 2 sts, K12 including st already on needle after cast (bind) off,* rep from * to * 5 times more, cast (bind) off 2 sts, K to end.
Next row Purl across row, casting on 2 sts to replace those cast (bound) off on previous row.
Work 6 rows in st st, beg with a K row.
Cast (bind) off loosely and evenly.

COLLAR

Cast on 121 sts, using 5½mm (US 9) needles and yarns KU.
Work 9 rows in K1, P1 rib in colour sequence given for back ribbing.
Keeping rib correct throughout, shape collar by casting (binding) off 4 sts at beg of next 2 rows and 3 sts at beg of next 24 rows, and AT THE SAME TIME cont in colour sequence given for back, then after 15 rows have been completed from beg, work one row more CM, 2 rows VVX, one row K, 2 rows BBT, 2 rows PUU, 2 rows SUU, one row BB, one row KU, 3 rows BOT, 2 rows HHT and 4 rows AORU. (41 sts).
Cast (bind) off evenly in rib, using AORU.

FINISHING

Join sleeve seams and side seams above and below pockets, using backstitch for main knitting and an edge to edge st for ribbing.
Fold front bands to WS along foldline and slip stitch loosely in place.
Attach shaped edge of collar to neck edge, fixing the straight row ends of collar to cast (bound) off sts at centre front.
Fold pocket edgings to WS along foldline and slip stitch loosely in place.
Slip stitch pocket linings loosely to WS of fronts.
Sew buttons to button band to correspond with buttonholes.
Press seams.

The Big Diamond jacket merges here with the elegantly decaying kitchen garden of Kentwell Hall in Suffolk.

RED SAILS

Because cottons don't usually have the textural interest of some wools I was tempted to mix two fine strands of different colours together to create 'marles' of tone. When I finished this design it suggested boats with red sails. The palette for Rowan cottons has been getting more and more subtle and rich in tone – these browny reds, oranges and pinks really get me going. I wear this often, especially in winter (in overheated houses it is quite comfortable).

SIZE AND MEASUREMENTS
One size to fit up to 107cm (42in) bust/chest
Finished measurement at underarm 128cm (50½in)
Length from shoulder 59cm (23¼in)
Sleeve length 49cm (19¼in)

YARN
Rowan Cotton Glacé, Sea Breeze, Cabled Mercerised Cotton, and Handknit DK Cotton – all 50g (1¾oz) balls

			Shade no	Amount
A	Glacé	Matador	742	2 balls
B	Glacé	Provence	744	1 ball
C	Glacé	Harebell	732	1 ball
D	Glacé	Dijon	739	1 ball
E	Glacé	Rowan	736	1 ball
F	Sea Brze	Catmint	556	2 balls
G	Sea Brze	Truffle	558	2 balls
H	Sea Brze	Madeira	565	1 ball
J	Merc Cott	Saffron	336	2 balls
L	Merc Cott	Firethorn	337	2 balls
M	Merc Cott	Geranium	338	2 balls
N	Merc Cott	Cerise	326	1 ball
O	DK Cott	Azure	248	2 balls
Q	DK Cott	Mango	262	2 balls
R	DK Cott	Port	245	2 balls
S	DK Cott	Olive	247	2 balls
T	DK Cott	Tope	253	2 balls
U	DK Cott	Raspberry	240	2 balls

Note: The finer yarns are used in combination, e.g. NN means use 2 strands of yarn N, AE means use one strand of yarn A and one strand of yarn E.
Yarns are shown on the chart by their relevant letters.

NEEDLES
Pair of 3¼mm (UK no 10) (US 3) needles
Pair of 4mm (UK no 8) (US 6) needles

TENSION/GAUGE
20 sts and 30 rows to 10cm (4in) measured over patterned st st using 4mm (US 6) needles.

Check your tension (gauge) carefully before beginning and change needle size if necessary.

NOTES
When working the colourwork pattern, use the intarsia method, using a separate length of yarn for each area of contrasting colour and linking one colour to the next by twisting them around each other where they meet on WS to avoid holes.
Read chart from right to left for K (RS odd-numbered) rows and from left to right for P (WS even-numbered) rows.

BACK
Cast on 100 sts, using 3¼mm (US 3) needles, and yarn U.
Work 27 rows in K1, P1 rib in the foll colour sequence:
One row U, 2 rows DG, one row LL, 3 rows R, one row O, one row JJ, 2 rows DD, 2 rows S, one row Q, 3 rows LM, one row FF, one row T, 2 rows JJ, one row S, 3 rows BD and 2 rows HH.
Next row (inc) (WS) Using yarn O, P3, (pick up horizontal loop before next st and purl into back of it — called *make one purlwise* or *M1p* —, P3, M1p, P4) 13 times, (M1p, P3) twice. (128 sts)
Change to 4mm (US 6) needles and cont in patt from chart (see Notes) for back which is worked entirely in st st, beg with a K row. **
Work 150 rows in patt, marking each end of row 66 for position of sleeve.
Cast (bind) off evenly.

FRONT
Work as given for back to **.
Work 90 rows in patt from chart for front, marking each end of row 66 for position of sleeve, so ending with a WS row.
Shape front neck
Chart row 91 (RS) Work 63 sts in patt, then turn and leave rem sts on a st holder.
Work each side of neck separately, foll chart throughout.
Work one row without shaping.
Dec one st at neck edge on next row and every foll alt row until 43 sts rem.
Cont without shaping until front matches back to shoulder.
Cast (bind) off evenly.
With RS facing, rejoin yarn to rem sts, cast (bind) off centre 2 sts, work in patt to end.
Complete to match first side of neck, reversing all shaping.

The browny-reds, oranges and pinks of the Red Sails V-neck sweater are brought stunningly to life against these weathered coral tones.

SLEEVES (both alike)
Cast on 50 sts, using 3¼mm (US 3) needles and yarn U.
Work 27 rows in K1, P1 rib in colour sequence as given for back.

Next row (inc) (WS) Using yarn O, P5, (M1p, P3) 13 times, M1p, P6. (64 sts)
Change to 4mm (US 6) needles and work 120 rows in patt from chart between markers for sleeve, and AT THE SAME TIME shape sides of

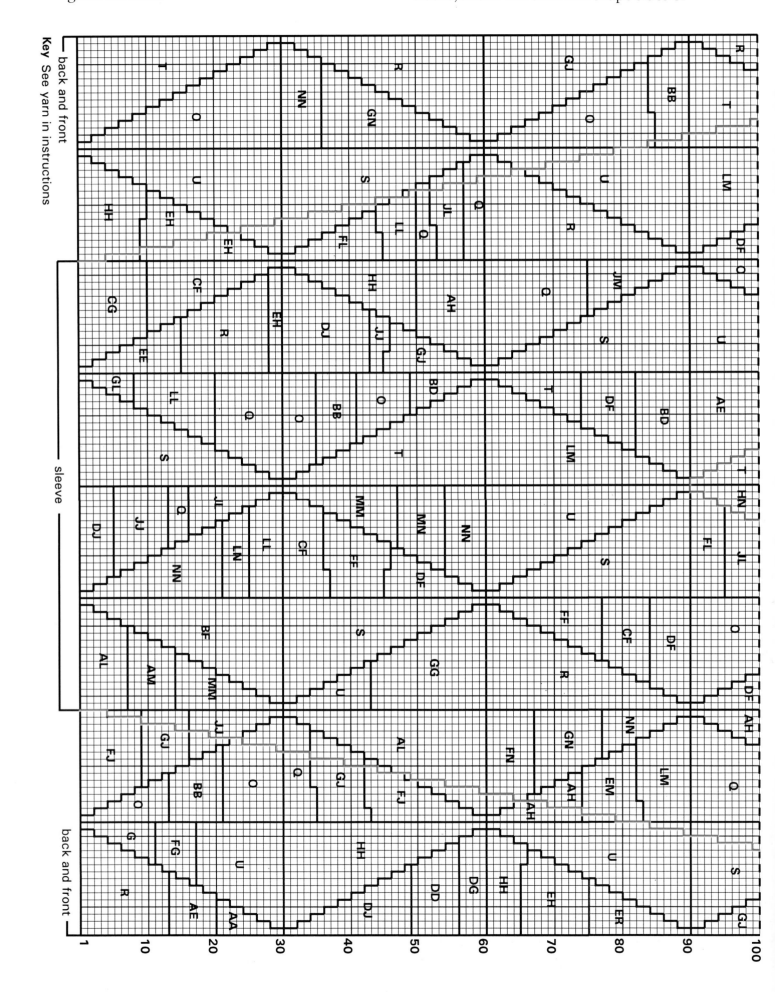

sleeve by inc one st at each end of 5th row and then inc one st at each end of every foll 5th row until there are 106 sts in all, taking extra sts into patt as they occur.
Cast (bind) off evenly.

NECKBAND

Press all pieces gently on WS, using a warm iron over a damp cloth and avoiding ribbing.
Join right shoulder seam, using backstitch.
With RS facing, using 3¼mm (US 3) needles and yarn U, pick up and K65 sts evenly down left front neck, 65 sts up right front neck and 38 sts across back neck. (168 sts)
Keeping colour sequence as listed below, work in K1, P1 rib as foll:
Row 1 (WS) Beg with a K st, rib 101 sts, P2tog, P2tog tbl, rib to end.
Row 2 Rib 62 sts, K2tog, tbl, K2tog, rib to end.
Cont in this way dec at centre on every row and when complete cast (bind) off evenly in rib.
Colour sequence: one row U, 2 rows GU, one row LL, 3 rows R, one row O, one row JJ, 2 rows D, 2 rows S, one row Q, 3 rows LM, one row FF, one row T, 2 rows JJ, one row S and one row O.

FINISHING

Use backstitch for all seams on main knitting and an edge to edge st for ribbing.
Join left shoulder seam and neckband.
Set in sleeves between markers.
Join side and sleeve seams.
Press seams.

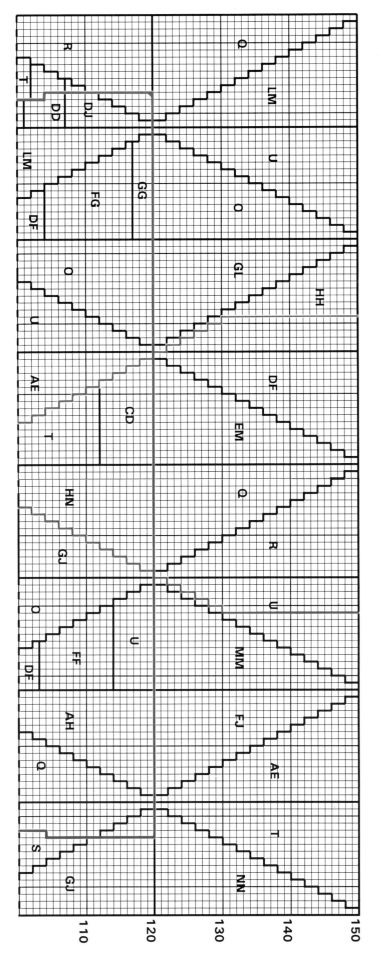

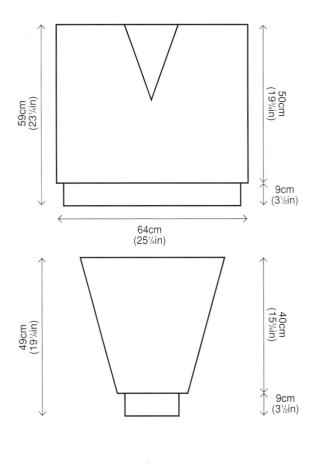

KILIM

A faded old woven carpet from Istanbul in Turkey caught my eye one day and led to this jacket. Combining beige and grey tweedy yarns with the greens, lavenders and golds, it really captures the worn feel of old weaving. The colouring has a timeless quality that the original carpet possesses.

SIZE AND MEASUREMENTS
One size to fit up to 122cm (48in) bust/chest
Finished measurement at underarm 161cm (63½in)
Length from shoulder 70cm (27¾in)
Sleeve length 42cm (16½in)

YARN
Rowan Kid Silk – 50g (1¾oz) balls, Rowanspun Tweed – 100g (3½oz) hanks, Designer DK – 50g (1¾ oz) balls, Lightweight DK – 25g (1oz) hanks, Fox Tweed DK – 50g (1¾oz) hanks, Chunky Cotton Chenille – 100g (3½oz) hanks, Donegal Lambswool Tweed – 25g (1oz) hanks, Wool/Cotton – 40g (1½oz) balls, and Botany – 25g (1oz) hanks

			Shade no	Amount
A	Kid Silk	Turnip	997	1 ball
B	Kid Silk	Old Gold	989	2 balls
C	Rid Silk	Smoke	998	2 balls
D	Kid Silk	Silver Blonde	995	2 balls
E	Rowanspun	Caper	762	1 hank
F	Kid Silk	Goat Brown	994	5 balls
F	Don Twd	Bramble	484	3 hanks
G	Ltwt DK		148	5 hanks
H	Don Twd	Nutmeg	470	2 hanks
J	Ltwt DK		5	3 hanks
K	Don Twd	Sedge	471	1 hank
L	Don Twd	Shale	467	4 hanks
M	Ltwt DK		63	3 hanks
N	Don Twd	Mist	466	2 hanks
O	Don Twd	Leaf	481	2 hanks
P	Ltwt DK		86	3 hanks
q	Ltwt DK		605	3 hanks
R	Ltwt DK		65	3 hanks
S	Ltwt DK		61	3 hanks
T	Ltwt DK		412	2 hanks
U	Fox Twd	Cricket	851	1 hank
V	Kid Silk	Potpourri	996	2 balls
W	Don Twd	Rye	474	1 hank
Y	Ltwt DK		54	1 hank
a	Fox Twd	Seal	852	1 hank
b	Ltwt DK		624	2 hanks
d	Don Twd	Bark	475	3 hanks
e	Don Twd	Elderberry	490	2 hanks
f	Des DK		616	1 ball
g	Kid Silk	Garnet	992	1 ball
h	Wool/Cott	Kashmir	910	2 balls
j	Don Twd	Pepper	473	5 hanks
m	Ltwt DK		64	3 hanks
n	Botany		118	2 hanks
r	Ch Chen	Wild Cherry	370	1 hank
t	Don Twd	Taragon	477	1 hank
y	Fox Twd	Wren	850	2 hanks

Note: The finer yarns are used in combination, e.g. SS means use 2 strands of yarn S, Za means use one strand of yarn Z and one strand of yarn a. Yarns are shown on the charts either by their relevant letters or by symbols. Refer to the chart key for symbols.
Note that yarn F is one strand of Kid Silk (994) and one strand of Donegal Tweed (484) used together.

NEEDLES AND BUTTONS
Pair of 5mm (UK no 6) (US 8) needles
Pair of 6mm (UK no 4) (US 10) needles
Five buttons

TENSION/GAUGE
15 sts and 20 rows to 10cm (4in) measured over patterned st st using 6mm (US 10) needles.
Check your tension (gauge) carefully before beginning your knitting and change needle size if necessary.

NOTES
When working the colourwork pattern, use the intarsia method, using a separate length of yarn for each area of contrasting colour and linking one colour to the next by twisting them around each other where they meet on WS to avoid holes.
Read charts from right to left for K (RS odd-numbered) rows and from left to right for P (WS even-numbered) rows.

BACK
Cast on 92 sts, using 5mm (US 8) needles and yarns FR (see Note about yarn F).
Work 17 rows in K1, P1 rib in the foll colour sequence:
2 rows GF, 2 rows GMd, 2 rows jjmhn (symbol X), 2 rows JPB, one row BT, 3 rows Cd, one row OQ, one row Fe, 2 rows fG and one row Re.
Next row (inc) (WS) Using yarns Re, rib 4, (pick up horizontal loop before next st and work into back of it — called *make one* or *M1* —, rib 3) 29 times, rib 1. (121 sts)

The tweedy greys and beiges combined with greens, lavenders and golds of the Kilim jacket (left) are inspired by the colours of a faded old Turkish carpet. The Kilim jacket is shown together with the Baclava jacket (see page 26).

Key

- Yj
- jjmhn
- r
- LR
- MN
- LLL
- ad
- KKK
- FL
- Ra
- bdd
- Re
- JJP
- PP
- RR
- JJN
- SS
- RV
- LLS
- Fy
- Gv
- Dg
- fL
- Nf
- ag
- BH
- Nq
- Td
- HV
- LSe
- Kq
- NN
- Hq

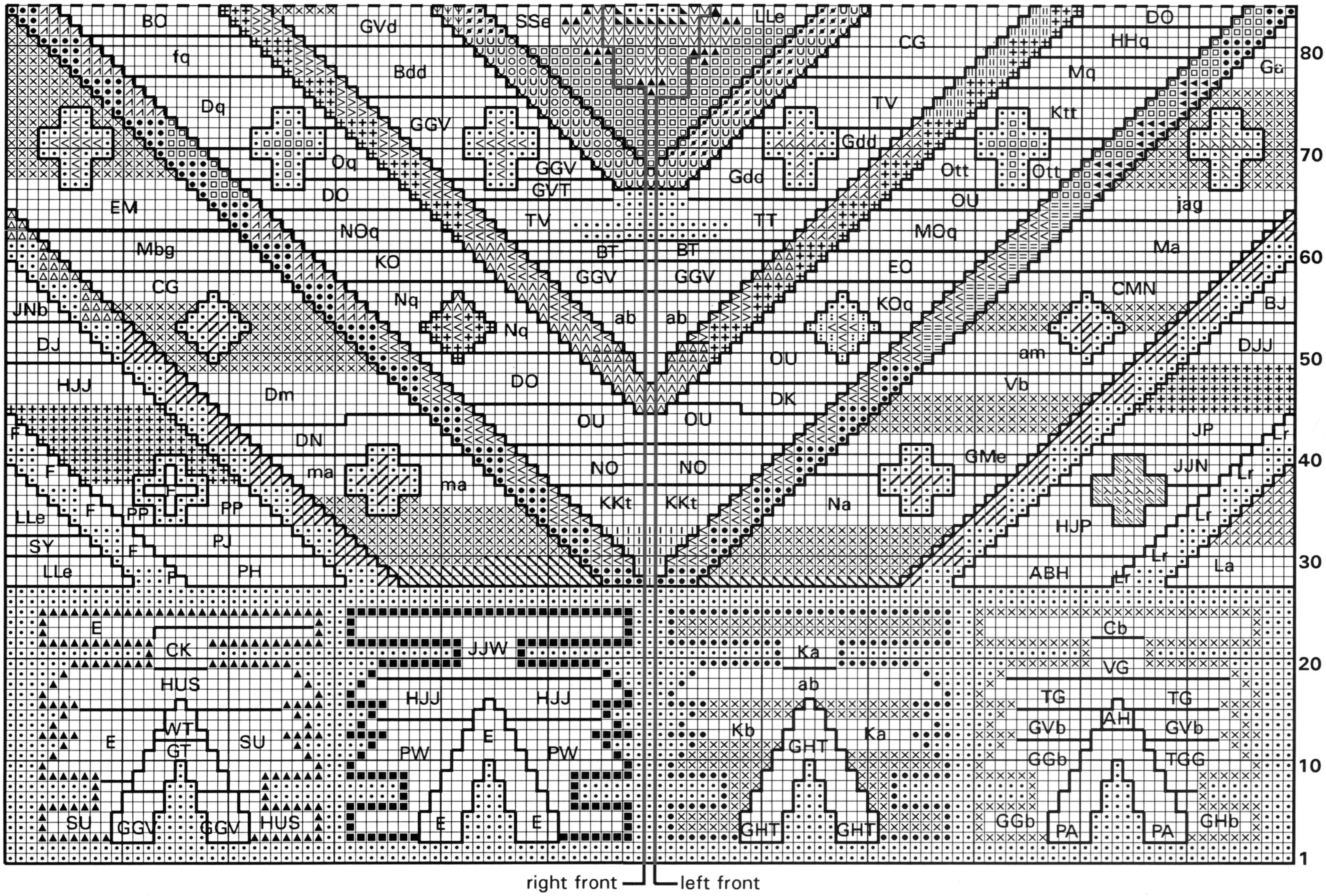

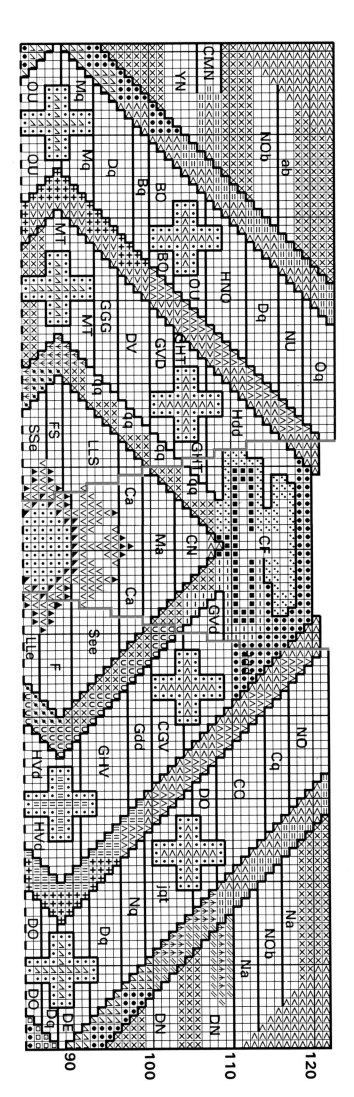

Change to 6mm (US 10) needles and cont in patt from chart (see Notes) for back which is worked entirely in st st, beg with a K row.

Work 120 rows in patt, marking each end of rows 12 and 46 for pocket openings, so ending with a WS row.

Shape back neck

Chart row 121 (RS) Work 52 sts in patt, then turn and leave rem sts on a st holder.

Work each side of neck separately, foll chart throughout.

Cast (bind) off 4 sts at beg of next row.

Cast (bind) off rem 48 sts.

With RS facing, rejoin yarn to rem sts, cast (bind) off centre 17 sts, work in patt to end.

Work one row without shaping.

Complete to match first side of neck, reversing all shaping.

LEFT FRONT

Cast on 46 sts, using 5mm (US 8) needles and yarns FR.

Work 17 rows in K1, P1 rib as given for back.

Next row (inc) (WS) Using yarns Re, rib 3, (M1, rib 3) 14 times, rib 1. (60 sts)

Change to 6mm (US 10) needles and work 75 rows in patt from chart between markers for left front, marking positions of pocket opening on side edge as for back, so ending with a RS row.

Shape front neck

Foll chart throughout, cast (bind) off 3 sts at beg of next row.

Work 3 rows without shaping.

Dec one st at beg of next row and every foll 4th row until 48 sts rem.

Work without shaping until front matches back to shoulder, ending with a WS row.

Cast (bind) off evenly.

RIGHT FRONT

Work as given for left front, reversing all shaping and foll chart between markers for right front.

SLEEVES (both alike)

Cast on 31 sts, using 5mm (US 8) needles and yarns FR.

Work 17 rows in K1, P1 rib as given for back.

Next row (inc) (WS) Using yarns Re, rib 3, (M1, rib 2) 14 times. (45 sts)

Change to 6mm (US 10) needles and work 64 rows in patt from chart for sleeve, and AT THE SAME TIME shape sides by inc one st at each end of 3rd row and every foll alt row until there are 97 sts, taking extra sts into patt as they occur.

Cast (bind) off loosely and evenly.

POCKET EDGINGS (both alike)

Press all pieces gently on WS, using a warm iron over a damp cloth and avoiding ribbing.

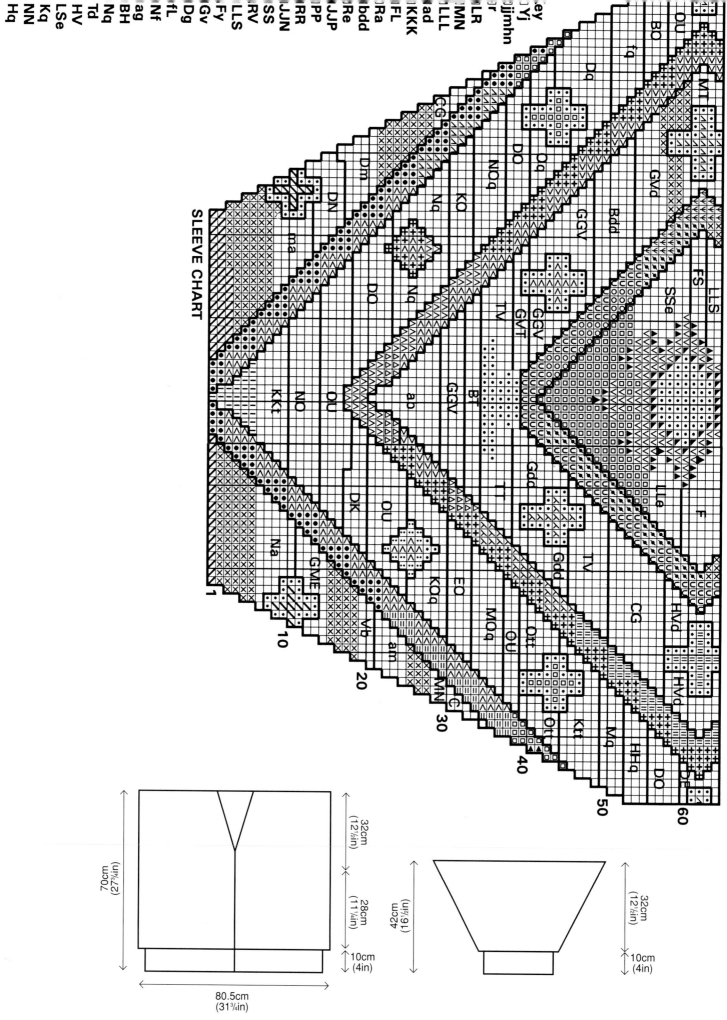

SLEEVE CHART

70cm
(27¾in)

80.5cm
(31¾in)

32cm
(12½in)

28cm
(11¼in)

10cm
(4in)

42cm
(16¾in)

32cm
(12½in)

10cm
(4in)

24

With RS facing, using 5mm (US 8) needles and yarn f, pick up and K30 sts evenly between markers on side edge of front.
K one row (WS) to form foldline.
Work 4 rows in st st, beg with a K row.
Cast (bind) off loosely and evenly.

POCKET LININGS

With RS facing, using 6mm (US 10) needles and yarn f, pick up and K31 sts evenly between markers on left side edge of back and work in st st, beg with a P row, and AT THE SAME TIME shape pocket lining by casting on 8 sts at beg of first row and dec one st at end of 5th row and then dec one st at end of every foll alt row until 24 sts rem in all.
Cast (bind) off evenly.
Work right pocket lining as given for left pocket lining, reversing all shaping.

BUTTONHOLE BAND

With RS facing, using 5mm (US 8) needles and yarns FR, pick up and K67 sts evenly along right front edge for a woman's jacket or along left front edge for a man's, leaving shaped neck edge unworked.
Next row (buttonhole) (WS) P4,* cast (bind) off 2 sts, P13 including st already on needle after cast (bind) off,* rep from * to * 3 times more, cast (bind) off 2 sts, P3.
Next row Knit across row, casting on 2 sts to replace those cast (bound) off on previous row.
K one row to form foldline.
Work 8 rows in st st, beg with a K row and AT THE SAME TIME work buttonholes on rows 2 and 3 to correspond with those already made.
Cast (bind) off loosely and evenly.

BUTTON BAND

Work on other front as given for buttonhole band, omitting buttonholes.

COLLAR

Cast on 133 sts, using 5mm (US 8) needles and yarns FR.
Cont in K1, P1 rib in colour sequence outlined below, and AT THE SAME TIME shape collar by casting (binding) off 4 sts at beg of 7th row and every foll row until 17 sts rem.
Colour sequence: 2 rows FG, 2 rows GMd, 2 rows jjmhn, 2 rows JPB, one row BT, 3 rows Cd, one row OQ, one row Fe, 2 rows fG, 3 rows LRe, 2 rows CRG, 3 rows jjmhn, 3 rows BOe, 2 rows FR, one row Wdd, 4 rows SeL and 2 rows GVd.
Cast (bind) off loosely in rib, using yarns GVd.

FINISHING

Use backstitch for seams on all main knitting and an edge to edge st for ribbing.
Join both shoulder seams.
Fold front bands to WS along foldline and slip stitch loosely in place.
Attach shaped edge of collar neatly to neckline, with centre back of cast (bound) off row at centre back neck and cast on edge of collar and foldlines of front bands in one continuous line.
Place markers 32cm (13in) down from shoulder seam on back and fronts.
Set in sleeves between markers. Join sleeve seams and side seams above and below pockets.
Fold pocket edgings to WS along foldline and slip stitch loosely in place.
Slip stitch pocket linings loosely to WS of fronts.
Sew on buttons to correspond with buttonholes.
Press seams.

BACLAVA

An Anatolian woven carpet jumped off the page of a book on kilims that I purchased lately. The small trapezoid shapes making up the bold diamonds of the all-over pattern reminded me of Greek honey cakes. Of all my recent work, this is the most fascinating to knit: every so many rows a new colour comes in and everything shifts on a few stitches so that the knitter is always experiencing change as the piece grows.

SIZES AND MEASUREMENTS

To fit 91–97[102–112:117–122]cm
(36–38[40–44:46–48]in) bust/chest
Finished measurement at underarm
132[136:143]cm (52 [53½:56½]in)
Length from shoulder 68cm (26¾in)
Sleeve length 43cm (17¼in)
*Figures for larger sizes are given in brackets [];
where there is only one set of figures, it applies to
all sizes.*

YARN

Rowan Donegal Lambswool Tweed and Kid Silk –
both 25g (1oz) hanks/balls

			Shade no	Amounts
A	Don Twd	Roseberry	480	6[6:7] hanks
B	Don Twd	Dolphin	478	4[5:5] hanks
C	Don Twd	Sedge	471	2[3:3] hanks
D	Don Twd	Leaf	481	1[1:1] hank
E	Don Twd	Tarragon	477	2[3:3] hanks
F	Don Twd	Pickle	483	1[1:2] hanks
G	Don Twd	Cinnamon	479	2[3:3] hanks
H	Don Twd	Pepper	473	1[1:1] hank
J	Kid Silk	Old Gold	989	2[3:3] balls
L	Don Twd	Rainforest	489	1[2:2] hanks
M	Don Twd	Elderberry	490	1[1:2] hanks
N	Don Twd	Mist	466	2[2:3] hanks
R	Don Twd	Storm	468	2[2:3] hanks
S	Don Twd	Marram	472	2[2:2] hanks
T	Don Twd	Rye	474	2[2:2] hanks
U	Don Twd	Bramble	484	1[1:2] hanks
V	Don Twd	Bay	485	1[1:1] hank
W	Kid Silk	Holly	990	3[4:4] balls
2	Kid Silk	Steel	991	2[2:2] balls
3	Kid Silk	Pot pourri	996	2[2:3] balls
4	Kid Silk	Smoke	998	1[1:2] balls

Note: Use all yarns doubled throughout.
Yarns are shown on the chart either by their
relevant letters or by symbols.

NEEDLES AND BUTTONS

Pair of 4mm (UK no 8) (US 6) needles
Pair of 5mm (UK no 6) (US 8) needles
Seven buttons

TENSION/GAUGE

17½ and 24 rows to 10cm (4in) measured over
patterned st st using 5mm (US 8) needles and
yarn doubled.
*Check your tension (gauge) carefully before
beginning and change needle size if necessary.*

NOTES

*When working the colourwork pattern, use the
intarsia method, using a separate length of yarn
for each area of contrasting colour, linking one
colour to the next by twisting them around each
other where they meet on WS to avoid holes.
Read chart from right to left for K (RS odd-
numbered) rows and from left to right for P (WS
even-numbered) rows.*

BACK

Cast on 86[90:96] sts, using 4mm (US 6) needles
and yarn A doubled.
Using yarn doubled throughout, work 19 rows in
K1, P1 rib in the foll colour sequence:
One row A, 2 rows B, one row C, one row D, one
row E, 2 rows F, one row G, one row C, 2 rows B,
one row J, one row A, one row C, 2 rows E, one
row L and one row M.
Next row (inc) (WS) Using yarn M, rib 1[3:6],
(pick up horizontal loop before next st and work
into back of it — called *make one* or *M1* —, rib 3)
28 times, M1, rib 1[3:6]. (115[119:125] sts)
Change to 5mm (US 8) needles and cont in patt
from chart (see Notes) for back which is worked
entirely in st st, beg with a K row.
Work 144 rows in patt, marking each end of rows
7 and 40 for pocket openings and each end of
row 70 for position of sleeve, so ending with a WS
row.

Shape back neck

Chart row 145 (RS) Work 44[46:49] sts in patt,
then turn and leave rem sts on a st holder.
Work each side of neck separately, foll chart
throughout.
Cast (bind) off 4 sts at beg of next row.
Cast (bind) off rem 40[42:45] sts.
With RS facing, rejoin yarn to rem sts, cast (bind)
off centre 27 sts, work in patt to end.
Work one row without shaping.
Complete to match first side of neck, reversing all
shaping.

LEFT FRONT

Cast on 44[46:49] sts, using 4mm (US 6) needles
and yarn A doubled.
Using yarn doubled throughout, work 19 rows in
K1, P1 rib as given for back.
Next row (inc) (WS) Using yarn M, rib 1[2:3],
(M1, rib 3) 14 times, M1, rib 1[2:4]. (59[61:64] sts)
Change to 5mm (US 8) needles and work 79 rows
in patt from chart between markers for left front,

marking positions of pocket opening and sleeve on side edge as for back, so ending with a RS row.

Shape front neck

Foll chart throughout, cast (bind) off 3 sts at beg of next row.

Work 2 rows without shaping.

Dec one st at neck edge on next row and every foll 3rd row until there are 40[42:45] sts.

Work without shaping until front matches back to shoulder, ending with a WS row.

Cast (bind) off evenly.

RIGHT FRONT

Work as given for left front, reversing all shaping and foll chart between markers for right front.

SLEEVES (both alike)

Cast on 42 sts, using 4mm (US 6) needles and yarn A doubled.

Using yarns doubled throughout, work 19 rows in K1, P1 rib as given for back.

Next row (inc) (WS) Using yarn M, (rib 3, M1) 13 times, rib 3. (55 sts)

Change to 5mm (US 8) needles and work 86 rows in patt from chart between markers for sleeve, and AT THE SAME TIME shape sides by inc one st at each end of 3rd row and every foll alt row 11 times, then every foll 3rd row until there are 111 sts, taking extra sts into patt as they occur.

Cast (bind) off loosely and evenly.

COLLAR

Cast on 150 sts, using 4mm (US 6) needles and yarn A doubled.

Using yarns doubled throughout, cont in K1, P1 rib in colour sequence outlined below, and AT THE SAME TIME shape collar by casting (binding) off 3 sts at beg of 11th row and every foll row until 42 sts rem.

Colour sequence: one row A, 2 rows B, one row C, 2 rows D, 2 rows E, 3 rows F, one row G, one row C, 2 rows B, 2 rows J, 2 rows A, one row C, 3 rows E, 2 rows L, 2 rows M, one row A, 2 rows B, one row C, 2 rows D, 2 rows E, 3 rows F, one row G, one row C, 2 rows B, 2 rows J and 2 rows A.

Cast (bind) off loosely and evenly in rib, using yarn A.

POCKET EDGINGS (both alike)

Press all pieces gently on WS, using a warm iron over a damp cloth and avoiding ribbing.

With RS facing, using 4mm (US 6) needles and yarn B doubled, pick up and K34 sts evenly between markers on side edge of front.

Using yarns doubled throughout, K one row to form foldline.

Work 4 rows in st st, beg with a K row.

Cast (bind) off loosely and evenly.

POCKET LININGS

With RS facing, using 5mm (US 8) needles and yarn B doubled, pick up and K34 sts evenly between markers on left side edge of back and work in st st, beg with a P row, and AT THE SAME TIME cast on 8 sts at beg of first row and dec one

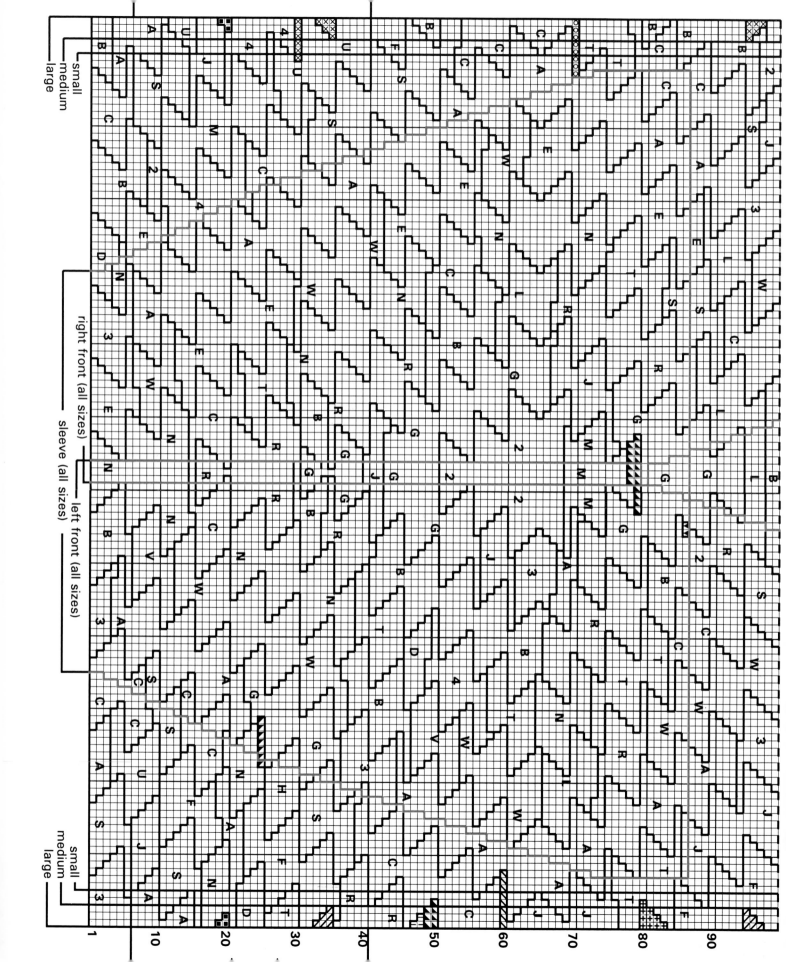

BUTTONHOLE BAND

With RS facing, using 4mm (US 6) needles and yarn B, pick up and K67 sts evenly along right front edge for woman's jacket or left front edge for a man's, leaving shaped neck edge unworked.

Next row (buttonhole) (WS) P2, *cast (bind) off 2 sts, P8 including st already on needle after cast (bind) off,* rep from * to * 5 times more, cast (bind) off 2 sts, P3.

Next row Knit across row, casting on 2 sts to replace those cast (bound) off on previous row. P one row.

Change to yarn A and K 2 rows to form foldline. Work 8 rows in st st, beg with a K row and work buttonholes on rows 2 and 3 to correspond with those already made.

Cast (bind) off loosely and evenly.

BUTTON BAND

Work on other front as given for buttonhole band, omitting buttonholes.

FINISHING

Use backstitch for all seams on main knitting and an edge to edge st for ribbing.

Join both shoulder seams.

Fold front bands to WS along foldline and slip stitch loosely in place.

Attach shaped edge of collar neatly to neckline, with centre back of cast (bound) off row at centre back neck and cast on edge of collar and foldlines in one continuous line.

Set in sleeves between markers.

Join sleeve seams and side seams above and below pockets.

Fold pocket edgings to WS along foldline and slip stitch loosely in place. Slip stitch pocket linings loosely to WS of fronts. Sew on buttons to correspond with buttonholes. Press seams.

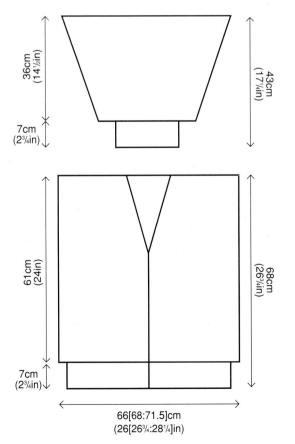

36cm (14½in)
43cm (17¼in)
7cm (2¾in)
61cm (24in)
68cm (26¾in)
7cm (2¾in)
66[68:71.5]cm (26[26¾:28¼]in)

100　　110　　120　　130　　140　146

BLUE DIAMOND

The original Red Diamond was inspired by Indian silk embroidery in shades of deep red. A child's version of it (from my *Family Album* book) can be seen on pages 36–7. When I came to redo the Red Diamond colourway I felt shades of blues and turquoises would be coolly exciting. I've also been wearing a lot of cotton all year round so felt a cotton version would be practical and comfortable to wear. This design, of course, would look good in any group of shades: beiges, purples, greens, pinks – I did one in dark bottle green and royal blues that worked a treat. The bright little centres lift the diamonds, so do make them strong and colourful in any experiments.

SIZE AND MEASUREMENTS

One size to fit up to 122cm (48in) bust/chest
Finished measurement at underarm 138cm (55in)
Length from shoulder 65cm (26in)
Sleeve length 41cm (16½in)

YARN

Rowan Handknit DK Cotton, Nice Cotton, and Cabled Mercerised Cotton – all 50g (1¾oz) balls

			Shade no	Amount
A	DK Cott	China	267	3 balls
B	DK Cott	Olive	247	5 balls
C	DK Cott	Royal	294	3 balls
D	Nice	Lilac Wine	440	4 balls
E	DK Cott	Kingfisher	273	2 balls
F	Nice	Airforce	442	2 balls
G	DK Cott	Tope	253	1 ball
H	Nice	Parakeet	433	2 balls
J	DK Cott	Azure	248	2 balls
L	DK Cott	Mango	262	1 ball
M	DK Cott	Port	245	1 ball
N	Merc Cott	Mauve Pink	333	1 ball
P	DK Cott	Scarlet	255	1 ball
R	DK Cott	Diana	287	3 balls

Note: Use Cabled Mercerised Cotton doubled throughout and other yarns single.
Yarns are shown on the chart either by their relevant letters or by symbols. Refer to the chart key for symbols.

NEEDLES

Pair of 3¼mm (UK no 10) (US 3) needles
Pair of 4mm (UK no 8) (US 6) needles
Set of four double-pointed needles 3¼mm (UK no 10) (US 3)
Set of four double-pointed needles 4mm (UK no 8) (US 6)

TENSION/GAUGE

21 sts and 25 rows to 10cm (4in) measured over patterned st st using 4mm (US 6) needles.
Check your tension (gauge) carefully before beginning and change needle size if necessary.

NOTES

The pattern is comprised of a series of interlocking diamond motifs. Use separate lengths of yarn (the intarsia method) for each diamond, linking one colour to the next by twisting them around each other where they meet on WS to avoid holes. Carry the outline colours, yarns G and B, loosely across the back of the work, weaving in every 3 or 4 sts and spreading sts to their correct width to keep them elastic (the fairisle method). Read chart from right to left for K (RS odd-numbered) rows and from left to right for P (WS even-numbered) rows.

BACK AND FRONT (one piece)

Beg at lower back edge, cast on 120 sts, using 3¼mm (US 3) needles and yarn E.
Work 15 rows in K1, P1 rib in the foll colour sequence:
2 rows C, one row H, 2 rows D, one row F, one row B, 2 rows J, one row R, one row N, one row F, 2 rows A and one row B.
Next row (inc) (WS) Using yarn B, rib 4, (pick up horizontal loop before next st and work into back of it — called *make one* or *M1* —, rib 5, M1, rib 4, M1, rib 5) 8 times, M1, rib 4. (145 sts)
Change to 4mm (US 6) needles and work in patt from chart (see Notes) for back which is worked entirely in st st, beg with a K row.
Work 144 rows in patt, so ending with a WS row.
Divide for neck
Chart row 145 (RS) Work 62 sts in patt, then turn and leave rem sts on a st holder.
Work each side of neck separately, foll chart throughout.
Cast (bind) off 5 sts at beg of next row and foll alt row. (52 sts)
Work 2 rows without shaping.
Mark each end of last row (chart row 150) for shoulder line.
From this point onwards work back down chart towards row 1, beg at row 149.
Work 14 rows in patt without shaping, so ending with a WS row.
Shape front neck
Inc one st at neck edge on next row and 8 foll alt rows. (61 sts)
Inc one st at neck edge on next 7 rows, so ending with a WS row. (68 sts)

The Blue Diamond cotton crewneck combines shades of blues and turquoises with pea-green.

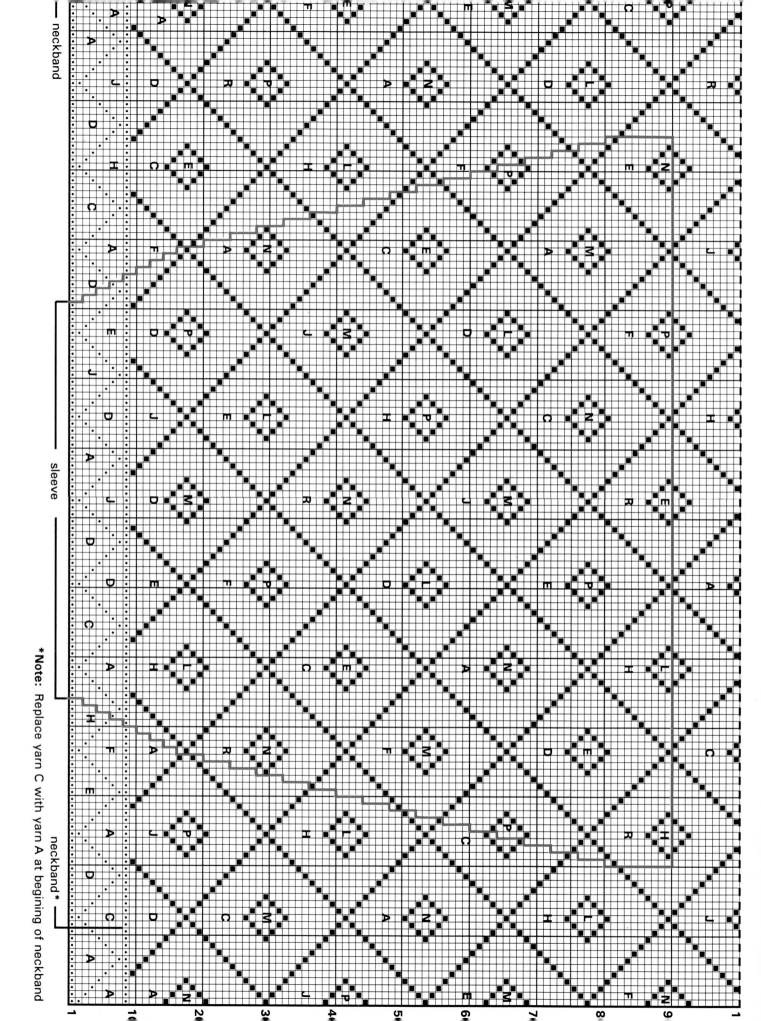

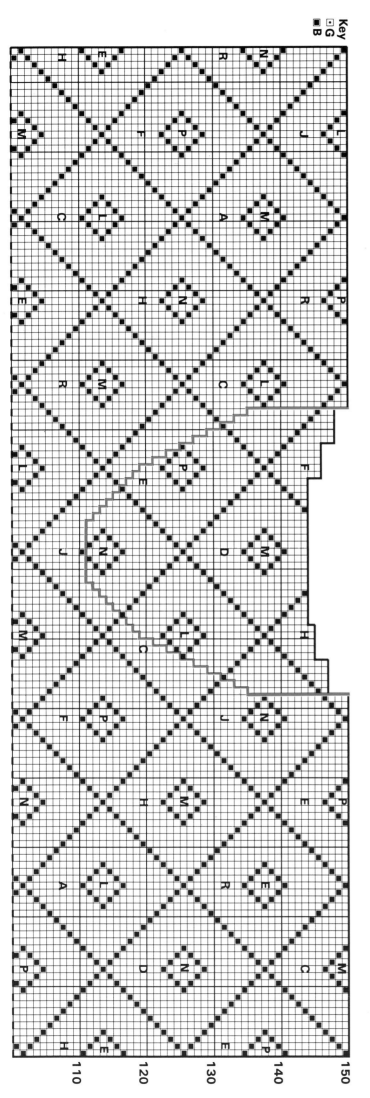

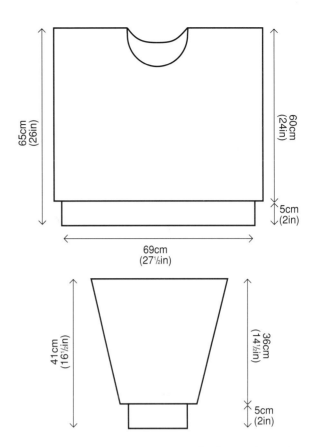

Leave these sts on a spare needle for right side front neck.

With RS facing, rejoin yarn to rem sts, cast (bind) off centre 21 sts, work in patt to end.

Work one row without shaping, then complete left side front neck to match right side, reversing all shaping and ending with a WS row.

Leave these sts on a spare needle for left side front neck.

Join right and left sides

Return to sts left on holder for right side front neck, rejoin yarn, work in patt across 68 sts, cast on 9 sts using yarn J, work in patt across 68 sts left on holder for left side front neck. (145 sts)

Work without shaping until chart row 1 has been completed, so ending with a RS row.

Change to 3¼mm (US 3) needles and work dec row as foll:

Next row (dec) (WS) Using yarn B, P6, (P2 tog, P3, P2 tog, P4) 12 times, P2 tog, P5. (120 sts)

Work 15 rows in K1, P1 rib, reversing colour sequence given for back.

Work one row in rib, using yarn E.

Cast (bind) off evenly in rib, using yarn E.

SLEEVES (both alike)

Cast on 50 sts, using 3¼mm (US 3) needles and yarn E.

Work 15 rows in K1, P1 rib in colour sequence as given for back.

Next row (inc) (WS) Using yarn B, rib 1, (M1, rib 8) 6 times, M1, rib 1. (57 sts)

Change to 4mm (US 6) needles and work 90 rows in patt from chart between markers for sleeve,

This cotton version of the Blue Diamond crewneck is practical and comfortable to wear all year round.

and AT THE SAME TIME shape sides by inc one st at each end of 3rd row and every foll alt row 8 times in all, then every foll 4th row until there are 105 sts, taking extra sts into patt as they occur. Cast (bind) off loosely and evenly.

NECKBAND

Press all pieces gently on WS, using a warm iron over a damp cloth and avoiding ribbing.
With RS facing, using 4mm (US 6) double-pointed needles and yarn G, beg at left shoulder line and pick up and K45 sts evenly down left from neck to centre front, 44 sts up right front neck to shoulder line and 45 sts across back neck. (134 sts)
Working back and forth in rows throughout and beg at row 2 of chart with a P row, work 7 rows in patt from chart between markers for neck border, so ending with chart row 8 (WS). Note that yarn C is replaced by yarn A on first triangle so that patt will match.
Change to 3¼mm (US 3) double-pointed needles and work in rounds as foll:
Next round (dec) (RS) Using yarn N, (K2, K2tog) 33 times, K2tog. (100 sts)
Work 7 rounds in K1, P1 rib in the foll colour sequence:
One round A, 2 rounds J, one round B, one round F and 2 rounds D.
Cast (bind) off evenly in rib, using yarn H.

FINISHING

Use backstitch for all seams on main knitting and an edge to edge st for ribbing.
Join neck border seam.
Place markers 25cm (10in) down from shoulder line on back and front.
Set in sleeves between markers.
Join side and sleeve seams. Press seams.

WINDOWS

This is one of my all-time favourites and proved to be a turning point for Rowan. I once proposed we produce an ambitious knitting kit with forty colours in it (the previous limit was twenty). When done, the fear was that the project would prove too expensive and time-consuming for the public – I'm delighted to report that the Windows coat was taken up with enthusiasm and became a best-seller a year later. This is a more up to date colourway that I hope you will find very wearable. You can gather the bottom as I have into a rib, or knit a hem and let the bottom swing out like an overcoat.

SIZE AND MEASUREMENTS
One size to fit up to 122cm (48in) bust
Finished measurement at underarm 188cm (74in)
Length from shoulder, with lower ribbing 107cm (42¼in) or with hem 100cm (39½in)
Sleeve length 34cm (13¼in)

YARN
Rowan Lambswool Tweed – 50g (1¾oz) balls, Rowanspun Tweed – 100g (3½oz) hanks, Magpie – 100g (3½oz) hanks, Donegal Lambswool Tweed – 25g (1oz) hanks, Kid Silk – 25g (1oz) balls, Lightweight DK – 25g (1oz) hanks

			Shade no	Amount
A	Rwnspn	Caper	762	5 hanks
B	Lbs Twd	Bluster	184	4 balls
C	Rwnspn	Tea	752	2 hanks
D	Magpie	Ivy	765	1 hank
E	Don Twd	Cinnamon	479	3 hanks
F	Don Twd	Bark	475	3 hanks
G	Don Twd	Pickle	483	2 hanks
H	Don Twd	Elderberry	490	2 hanks
J	Don Twd	Roseberry	480	2 hanks
L	Don Twd	Shale	467	1 hank
M	Don Twd	Juniper	482	2 hanks
N	Don Twd	Mist	466	1 hank
Q	Don Twd	Sapphire	486	2 hanks
R	Don Twd	Pepper	473	1 hank
S	Don Twd	Bramble	484	2 hanks
T	Don Twd	Nut	470	1 hank
U	Don Twd	Rye	474	1 hank
V	Don Twd	Sedge	471	1 hank
W	Don Twd	Rainforest	489	1 hank
X	Kid Silk	Pot Pourri	996	1 ball
Y	Kid Silk	Garnet	992	1 ball
Z	Kid Silk	Steel Blue	991	1 ball
a	Kid Silk	Violet Haze	982	1 ball
b	Kid Silk	Smoke	998	1 ball
C	Ltwt DK		90	1 hank
d	Ltwt DK		55	1 hank
e	Ltwt DK		501	2 hanks
f	Ltwt DK		27	2 hanks
g	Ltwt DK		77	1 hank
h	Des DK		667	1 ball
i	Ltwt DK		57	1 hank
j	Ltwt DK		65	2 hanks
k	Ltwt DK		99	1 hank
l	Ltwt DK		61	1 hank
m	Ltwt DK		72	1 hank
n	Ltwt DK		412	1 hank
q	Ltwt DK		71	1 hank
r	Ltwt DK		99	1 hank
t	Ltwt DK		125	1 hank
y	Magpie	Highland	118	1 hank

Note: The finer yarns are used in combination, e.g. Mj means use one strand of yarn M and one strand of yarn j, FFF means use 3 strands of F. Yarns are shown on the chart either by their relevant letters or by symbols.
*Yarn amounts have been estimated less generously for this coat, so that the knitter will have as little leftover yarn as possible. Extra yarn can be purchased later, if required, as matching dyelots is unnecessary.

NEEDLES
Pair of 5mm (UK no 6) (US 8) needles
Pair of 6mm (UK no 4) (US 10) needles
Circular needle 5mm (UK no 6) (US 8) 100cm (40in) long
Circular needle 6mm (UK no 4) (US 10) 100cm (40in) long

TENSION/GAUGE
16 sts and 20 rows to 10cm (4in) measured over patterned st st using 6mm (US 10) needles.
Check your tension (gauge) carefully before beginning and change needle size if necessary.

NOTES
The pattern is comprised of a series of interlocking rectangles (or 'windows'). Use separate lengths of yarn (the intarsia method) for each isolated block of colour, linking one colour to the next by twisting them around each other where they meet on WS to avoid holes.
The 'outline' sts separating each block of colour are worked throughout in yarn A. Carry the outline colour, yarn A, loosely across the back of the work, weaving in every 3 or 4 sts and spreading sts to their correct width to keep them elastic (the fairisle method).
Read charts from right to left for K (RS odd-numbered) rows and from left to right for P (WS even-numbered) rows unless otherwise stated.

Overleaf *The Windows coat (centre) with the Harlequin shawl-collar sweater (right) and the Red Diamond crewneck (both from* Family Album*).*

BACK, FRONTS AND SLEEVES (one piece)
Beg at lower edge of back, cast on 150 sts, using
6mm (US 10) needles and yarn A.
Work in patt from chart (see Notes) for back
which is worked entirely in st st, beg with a K row.
Work 150 rows in patt, marking each end of rows
100 and 130 for pocket openings, so ending with
a WS row.

Shape sleeves
Chart row 151 (RS) Using yarn A, cast on 34 sts,
work in patt across these 34 sts foll chart for right
sleeve, then work in patt across rem sts foll chart
for back, with a separate length of yarn A, cast on
34 sts onto LH needle, then work in patt across
these 34 sts foll chart for left sleeve. (218 sts)
Change to 6mm (US 10) circular needle to
accommodate the increased number of sts, then
work back and forth in rows throughout as follows.
Cont in patt foll all 3 charts until chart row 198
has been completed, so ending with a WS row.

Divide for fronts
Chart row 199 (RS) Work 101 sts in patt, then
turn and leave rem sts on a spare needle.
Work each front separately, foll chart throughout.
Change back to same size ordinary needles at this
stage, if desired.

Shape right back neck
Chart row 200 (WS) Cast (bind) off 6 sts, work in
patt to end. (95 sts)
Mark each end of last row for shoulder line.
From this point onwards work charts from top to
bottom, beg with chart row 200 which is now
read as a K row from right to left, and reading P
rows, which are now odd-numbered rows, from
left to right.
Work one row (chart row 200 as a K row) without
shaping.
Dec one st at beg (neck edge) of next row. (94 sts)
Work 5 rows without shaping, so ending with a
RS row.

Shape front neck
Inc one st at beg of next row (neck edge) and foll
alt row.
Work one row without shaping.
Cast on 2 sts at beg of next row, 4 sts at beg of foll
alt row and 7 sts at beg of foll alt row. (109 sts)
Cont on these sts only for right front, work
without shaping until sleeve matches back sleeve
from shoulder line (100 rows in all on sleeve),
ending at cuff edge.

Shape sleeve
Using yarn A, cast (bind) off 34 sts at beg of next
row. (75 sts)
Work without shaping until chart row 1 has been
completed, marking position of pocket opening
on side edge as for back, so ending with a WS
row.
Work one row without shaping, using yarn A.
Leave these sts on a spare needle.

With RS facing, rejoin yarn to rem sts, cast (bind)
off centre 16 sts, work in patt to end. (101 sts)
Complete left front to match right front,
reversing all shaping.

POCKET EDGINGS (both alike)
Press piece gently on WS, using a warm iron over
a damp cloth.
With RS facing, using 5mm (US 8) needles and
yarn C, pick up and K26 sts evenly between
pocket markers on side edge of front.
K one row (WS) to form foldline.
Work 4 rows in st st, beg with a K row.
Cast (bind) off loosely and evenly.

POCKET LININGS
With RS facing, using 6mm (US 10) needles and
yarn C, pick up and K25 sts evenly between
pocket markers on left side edge of back and
work in st st, beg with a P row, and AT THE SAME
TIME cast on 8 sts at beg of first row and dec one
st at end of 5th row (P row) and every foll P row
until 20 sts rem.
Cast (bind) off evenly.
Work right pocket lining as given for left pocket
lining, reversing all shaping.

CUFFS
With RS facing, using 5mm (US 8) needles and yarn
D, pick up and K52 sts evenly across sleeve end.
Work 25 rows in striped K1, P1 rib, working 4
rows D, 2 rows iY, 2 rows EX, 3 rows QSS, 3 rows
CJ, one row Ef, 2 rows ttt, 4 rows Sj, 2 rows
CS, one row Ef and one row JJJ, and AT THE SAME
TIME shape cuffs on the 5th, 10th, 15th and 20th
rows as foll:
5th row (WS) Using yarn iY, rib 5, P2 tog, (rib 8,
P2 tog) to last 5 sts, rib 5. (47 sts)
10th row (RS) Using yarn QSS, rib 4, K2 tog, (rib
7, K2tog) to last 5 sts, rib 5. (42 sts)
15th row (WS) Using yarn Ef, rib 4, K2tog tbl,
(rib 6, K2tog tbl) to last 4 sts, rib 4. (37 sts)
20th row (RS) Using yarn Sj, rib 3, P2 tog, (rib 5,
P2tog) to last 4 sts, rib 4. (32 sts)
Cast (bind) off loosely in rib, using yarn JJJ.

LOWER RIBBING OR HEM
Join sleeve and side seams above and below
pockets, using backstitch.
Either ribbing or a fold-up hem can be worked
along the lower edge of the coat.
Ribbing
For ribbing only, work as foll:
With RS facing, using 5mm (US 8) circular needle
and yarns QSS, pick up and K151 sts evenly along
bottom edge as foll:

The Windows coat, one of my all-time
favourites.

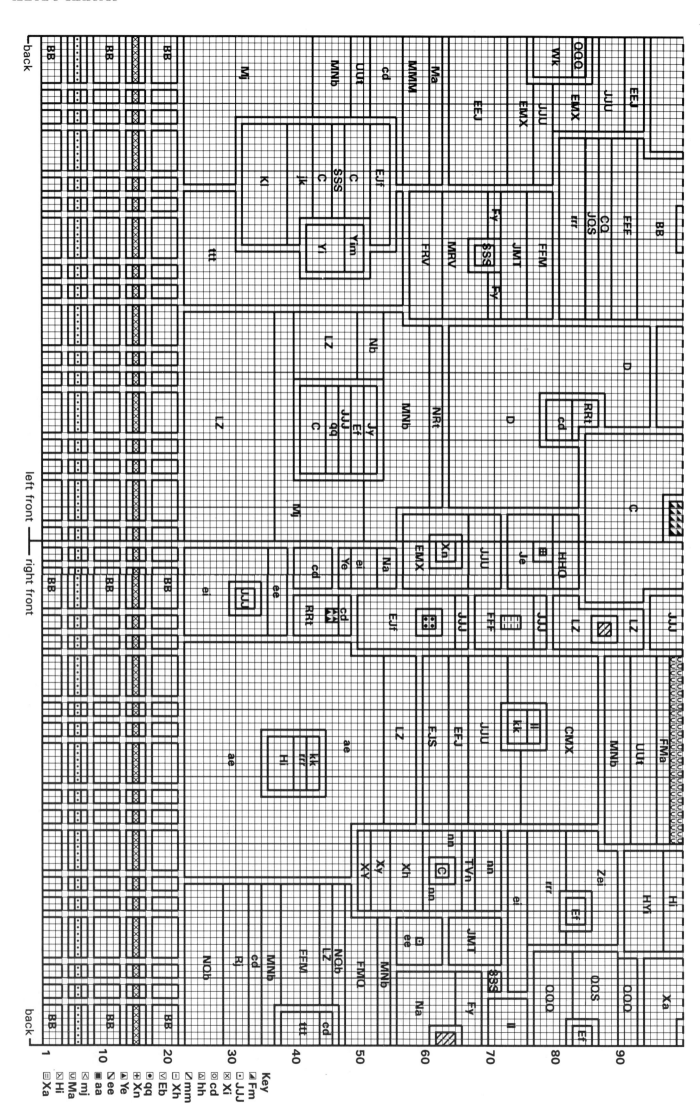

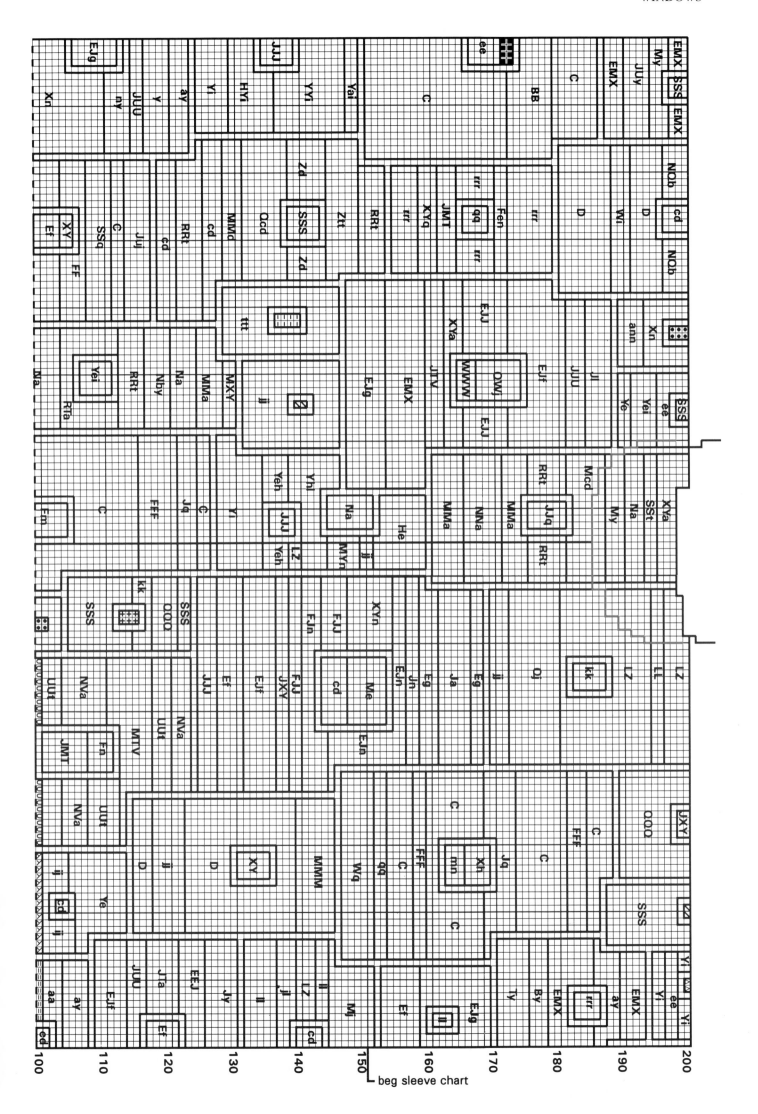

beg sleeve chart

From spare needle with left front sts (K2tog) 37 times, K1; pick up and K75 sts evenly along lower edge of back; from spare needle with right front sts K1, (K2tog) 37 times. (151 sts)
Working back and forth in rows, work 16 rows in K1, P1 rib in the foll colour sequence:
2 row QSS, 3 rows CJ, one row Ef, 2 rows ttt, 4 rows Sj, 2 rows CS, one row Ef and one row JJJ.
Cast (bind) off evenly in rib, using yarn JJJ.

Hem
For hem only, work as foll:
With RS facing, using 5mm (US 8) circular needlke and yarn C, K75 sts from spare needle with left front sts, pick up and K150 sts evenly along lower edge of back and K75 sts from spare needle with right front sts (300 sts)
**Working back and forth in rows throughout, K one row (WS) to form foldline.
Work 8 rows in st st, beg with a K row.
Cast (bind) off loosely.**
Fold hem to WS along foldline and slip st loosely in place.

FRONT EDGINGS (both alike)
For coat with lower ribbing work as foll:
With RS facing, using 5mm (US 8) circular needle and yarn C, pick up and K170 sts evenly along front edge, picking up about 3 sts for every 4 rows ends on ribbing and 6 sts for every 7 row ends on main knitting.
Work as for lower hem from ** to **.
Work front edgings for coat with hem in the same way as for coat with lower ribbing, but pick up 157 sts along front instead of 170.

COLLAR
Fold front edgings to WS along foldline and slip stitch loosely in place.
With RS facing, using 5mm (US 8) needles and yarn ESX, pick up and 90 sts evenly around neck edge.
Work 19 rows in K1, P1 rib, working (3 rows ESX, one row JJJ, 3 rows jj) twice, then 3 rows ESX and one row JJJ, and AT THE SAME TIME shape collar on 6th, 12th and 18th rows as foll:
6th row (RS) Rib 2, (K2tog tbl, rib 10) to last 4 sts, K2tog tbl, rib 2. (82 sts)
12th row (RS) Rib 2, (K2tog, rib 9) to last 3 sts, K2tog, rib 1. (74 sts)
18th row Rib 1, (P2tog, rib 8) to last 3 sts, P2tog, P1. (66 sts)
Cast (bind) off evenly in rib, using yarn JJJ.

FINISHING
Fold pocket edgings to WS along foldline and slip stitch loosely in place. Slip stitch pocket linings loosely to WS of fronts. Press seams.

Back view of the Windows coat.

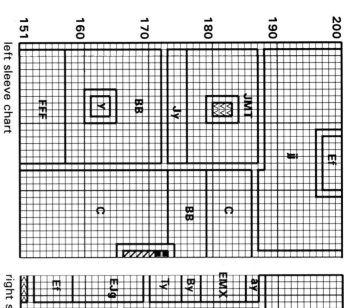

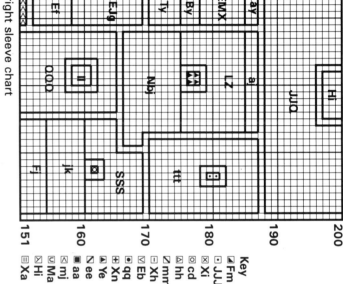

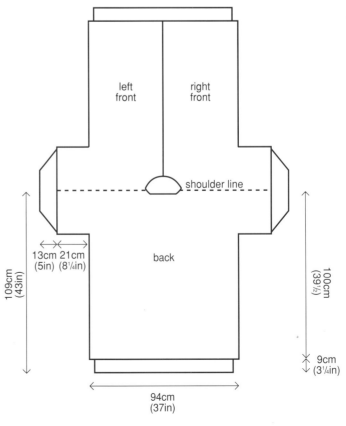

WHIRLING STAR

I've always loved tiles, particularly the intricate interlocking patterns of the Islamic world. These come from the famous tiles of the Alhambra in Granada, Spain. It is a delicious pattern to knit. As you will see in *Family Album*, I've produced many colourways for it. I'd be delighted to see other interpretations of this beautifully rhythmic design.

SIZE AND MEASUREMENTS
One size to fit up to 102cm (40in) bust/chest
Finished measurement at underarm 123cm (48½in)
Length from shoulder 63.5cm (25in)
Sleeve length 42.5cm (16¾in)

YARN
Rowan Lightweight DK – 25g (1oz) hanks

		Shade no	Amount
A	Ltwt DK	57	3 hanks
B	Ltwt DK	406	1 hank
C	Ltwt DK	90	1 hank
D	Ltwt DK	602	2 hanks
E	Ltwt DK	70	2 hanks
F	Ltwt DK	501	1 hank
G	Ltwt DK	91	3 hanks
H	Ltwt DK	46	2 hanks
J	Ltwt DK	99	2 hanks
K	Ltwt DK	77	2 hanks
L	Ltwt DK	54	2 hanks
M	Ltwt DK	73	2 hanks
N	Ltwt DK	407	2 hanks
O	Ltwt DK	55	1 hank
P	Ltwt DK	9	1 hank
R	Ltwt DK	404	1 hank
S	Ltwt DK	94	2 hanks
T	Ltwt DK	53	1 hank
W	Ltwt DK	62	3 hanks

Note: Yarns are shown on the chart either by their relevant letters or by symbols. Refer to the chart key for symbols.

NEEDLES
Pair 3¼mm (UK no 10) (US 3) needles
Pair 3¾mm (UK no 9) (US 5) needles

TENSION/GAUGE
25 sts and 32 rows to 10cm (4in) measured over patterned st st using 3¾mm (US 5) needles.
Check your tension (gauge) carefully before beginning and change needle size if necessary.

NOTES
When working the colourwork pattern, use the intarsia method, using a separate length of yarn for each area of contrasting colour and linking one colour to the next by twisting them around each other where they meet on WS to avoid holes. Read chart from right to left for K (RS odd-numbered) rows and from left to right for P (WS even-numbered) rows.

BACK
Cast on 132 sts, using 3¼mm (US 3) needles and yarn A.
Work 25 rows in K1, P1 rib in the foll colour sequence:
5 rows B, one row C, 3 rows D, one row E, one row F, 5 rows G, one row B, 3 rows A, one row H and 4 rows J.
Next row (inc) (WS) Using yarn J, rib 3, (pick up horizontal loop before next st and work into back of it — called *make one* or *M1* —, rib 6) 21 times, M1, rib 3. (154 sts)
Change to 3¾mm (US 5) needles and cont in patt from chart (see Notes) for back which is worked entirely in st st, beg with a K row. **
Work 182 rows in patt, so ending with a WS row.
Shape shoulders
Foll chart throughout, cast (bind) off 19 sts at beg of next 2 rows and 18 sts at beg of foll 4 rows.
Leave rem 44 sts on a st holder.

FRONT
Work as given for back to **.
Work 154 rows in patt from chart for front, so ending with a WS row.
Shape front neck
Chart row 155 (RS) Work 71 sts in patt, then turn and leave rem sts on a st holder.
Work each side of neck separately, foll chart throughout.
Cast (bind) off 3 sts at beg of next row and 2 sts at beg foll alt row.
Dec one st at neck edge on next row and every foll row until there are 55 sts.
Cont without shaping until front matches back to shoulder, ending with a WS row.
Shape shoulder
Cast (bind) off 19 sts at beg of next row and 18 sts at beg of foll alt row.
Work one row without shaping.
Cast (bind) off rem 18 sts.
With RS facing, return to rem sts, slip centre 12 sts onto a st holder, then rejoin yarn to rem sts, work in patt to end.
Work one row without shaping.
Complete to match first side of neck, reversing all shaping.

The Whirling Star crewneck glows against the brilliant red colour of one of Britain's few remaining old-style telephone boxes.

SLEEVES (both alike)
Cast on 65 sts, using 3¼mm (US 3) needles and yarn A.
Work 25 rows in K1, P1 rib in colour sequence as given for back.
Next row (inc) (WS) Using yarn J, rib 3, (M1, rib

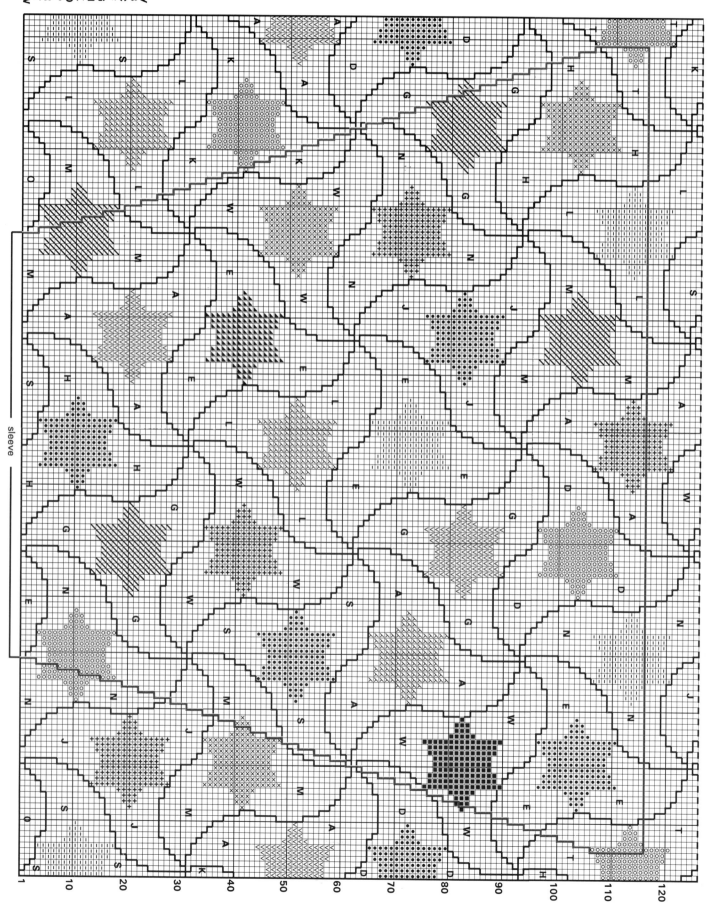

6) 10 times, M1, rib 2. (76 sts)
Change to 3¾mm (US 5) needles and work 116
rows in patt from chart between markers for
sleeve, and AT THE SAME TIME shape sides by inc
one st at each end of every 4th row until there
are 86 sts, then at each end of every foll 3rd row

until there are 144 sts, taking extra sts into patt as
they occur.
Cast (bind) off evenly.

NECKBAND

Press all pieces gently on WS, using a warm iron
over a damp cloth and avoiding ribbing
Join right shoulder seam, using backstitch.
With RS facing, using 3¼mm (US 3) needles and
yarn J, pick up and K35 sts evenly down left front
neck, K12 sts from st holder, pick up and K34 sts
up right front neck and K44 sts from st holder at
back neck. (125 sts)
Work 13 rows in K1, P1 rib in the foll colour
sequence:
4 rows J, one row H, 3 rows A, one row B and 4
rows G.
Cast (bind) off evenly in rib, using yarn G.

FINISHING

Use backstitch on all main knitting and an edge
to edge st on ribbing.
Join left shoulder seam and neckband.
Place markers 28.5cm (11½in) down from
shoulder seam on back and front.
Set in sleeves between markers.
Join side and sleeve seams.
Press seams.

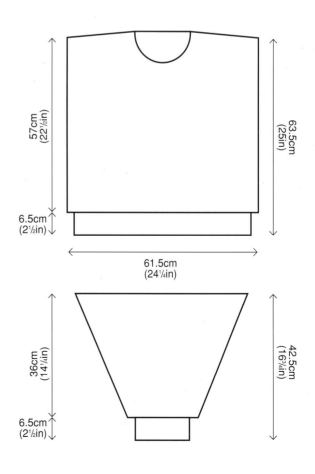

ANCIENT

I've often been moved by oriental landscapes with poems written over them in Chinese characters. This jacket suggests that effect with simple to knit little squares in place of words. The doubled yarns – wool and Kid Silk – give a luxurious subtlety of colour and texture. It's the sort of colouring that should blend elegantly with most landscapes.

SIZES AND MEASUREMENTS
To fit 91–97[102–112]cm (36–38[40–44]in) bust/chest
Finished measurement at underarm 115[128]cm (45[50½]in)
Length from shoulder 61.5[65.5]cm (24¼[25¾]in)
Sleeve length 46.5cm (18¼in)
Figures for larger size are given in brackets []; where there is only one set of figures, it applies to both sizes.

YARN
Rowan Kid Silk – 25g (1oz) balls, Donegal Lambswool Tweed – 25g (1oz) hanks, Designer DK – 50g (1¾oz) balls, Lambswool Tweed – 50g (1¾oz) balls, Fox Tweed DK – 50g (1¾oz) hanks, and Rowanspun Tweed – 100g (3½oz) hanks

			Shade no	Amount
A	Kid Silk	Old Gold	989	3[3] balls
B	Kid Silk	Steel Blue	991	2[2] balls
C	Kid Silk	Garnet	992	2[2] balls
D	Kid Silk	Violet Haze	982	1[2] balls
E	Kid Silk	Holly	990	1[1] ball
F	Kid Silk	Crushed Berry	993	1[1] ball
G	Kid Silk	Smoke	998	2[2] balls
H	Kid Silk	Potpourri	996	2[3] balls
J	Kid Silk	Silver Blonde	995	2[3] balls
L	Don Twd	Roseberry	480	2[3] hanks
N	Don Twd	Pickle	483	3[3] hanks
Q	Don Twd	Juniper	482	1[1] hank
R	Don Twd	Pepper	473	3[3] hanks
S	Don Twd	Nutmeg	470	3[3] hanks
T	Don Twd	Bay	485	1[1] hank
U	Don Twd	Cinnamon	479	1[1] hank
V	Des DK		616	2[2] balls
W	Des DK		65	1[1] ball
Y	Des DK		61	1[1] ball
Z	Des DK		671	1[1] ball
a	Don Twd	Bramble	484	2[2] hanks
b	Lbs Twd	Heliotrope	186	1[1] ball
e	Lbs Twd	Bluster	184	1[1] ball
f	Fox Twd	Hare	853	1[1] hank
g	Rwnspn	Tea	752	1[1] hank

Note: The finer yarns are used in combination, e.g. SS means use 2 strands of yarn S, Za means use one strand of yarn Z and one strand of yarn a.

Yarns are shown on the charts either by their relevant letters or by symbols. Refer to the chart key for symbols.

NEEDLES AND BUTTONS
Pair of 5mm (UK no 6) (US 8) needles
Pair of 5½mm (UK no 5) (US 9) needles
Pair of 6mm (UK no 4) (US 10) needles
Six buttons

TENSION/GAUGE
16 sts and 20 rows to 10cm (4in) measured over patterned st st using 6mm (US 10) needles.
Check your tension (gauge) carefully before beginning and change needle size if necessary.

NOTES
The pattern is comprised of a series of interlocking shaded patches upon which are superimposed lines of squares. Use separate lengths of yarn (the intarsia method) for the patches, linking one colour to the next by twisting them around each other where they meet on WS to avoid holes.
Carry the yarns used for the squares loosely across the back of the work, weaving in every 3 or 4 sts (the fairisle method).
Read charts from right to left for K (RS odd-numbered) rows and from left to right for P (WS even-numbered) rows.

BACK
Cast on 73[81] sts, using 5mm (US 8) needles and yarns Na.
Work 21 rows in K1, P1 rib in the foll colour sequence:
2 rows Na, one row g, 2 rows Le, one row LV, one row JR, 2 rows BZ, one row BW, one row QW, one row QY, one row QR, one row JR, one row Zb, 2 rows Cb, one row CY, one row DY, one row DR and one row Za.
Small size only:
Next row (inc) (WS) Using yarns Za, P5, (pick up horizontal loop before next st and purl into back of it — called *make one st purlwise* or *M1p* —, P3, M1p, P4) 9 times, M1p, P5. (92 sts)
Large size only:
Next row (inc) (WS) Using yarns Za, P1, (M1p, P4) 19 times, M1p, P3, M1p, P1. (102 sts)
Both sizes:
Change to 6mm (US 10) needles and cont in patt from chart (see Notes) for back which is worked entirely in st st, beg with a K row.
Work 106[114] rows in patt, marking each end of rows 7 and 36 for pocket openings, so ending

The Ancient jacket (left), with the Whirling Star waistcoat (from Kaffe's Colour Book from Rowan Yarns).

with a WS row.
Shape shoulders
Foll chart throughout, cast (bind) off 16[19] sts at beg of next 2 rows and 16[18] sts at beg of foll 2 rows.
Cast (bind) off rem 28 sts for back neck.

LEFT FRONT
Cast on 37[41] sts, using 5mm (US 8) needles and yarns Na.
Work 21 rows in K1, P1 rib as given for back.

Small size only:
Next row (inc) (WS) Using yarns Za, P2, (M1p, P3, M1p, P4) 5 times. (47 sts)
Large size only:
Next row (inc) (WS) Using yarns Za, P1, (M1p, P4) 9 times, M1p, P3, M1p, P1. (52 sts)
Both sizes:
Change to 6mm (US 10) needles and work 55[63] rows in patt from chart between markers for left front, marking positions of pocket opening on side edge as for back, so ending with a RS row.

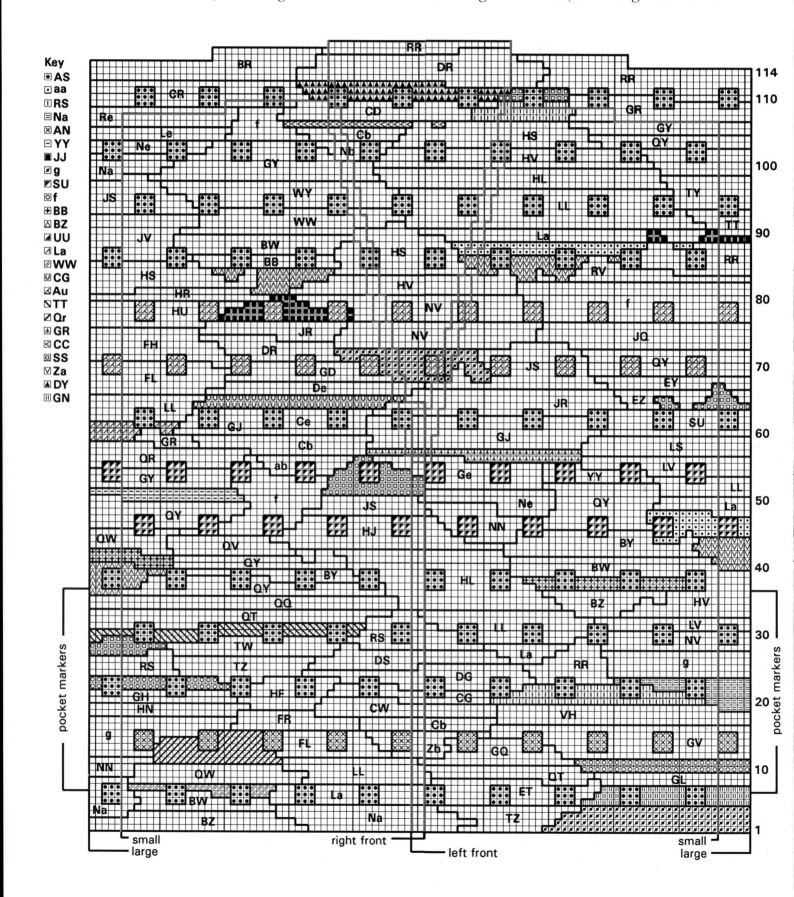

Key
- ⊡ AS
- ☐ aa
- ⊞ RS
- ⊟ Na
- ⊠ AN
- ⊡ YY
- ▣ JJ
- ▨ g
- ▤ SU
- ⊙ f
- ⊞ BB
- ◺ BZ
- ◿ UU
- ◹ La
- ▨ WW
- ⊔ CG
- ◩ Au
- ◺ TT
- ◿ Qr
- ◩ GR
- ◁ CC
- ⊡ SS
- ▽ Za
- ◭ DY
- ⫴ GN

Shape front neck

Foll chart throughout, cast (bind) off 3 sts at beg of next row.

Work 3 rows without shaping.

Dec one st at beg of next row and every foll 4th row until 32[37] sts rem.

Work without shaping until front matches back to shoulder, ending with a WS row.

Shape shoulder

Cast (bind) off 16[19] sts at beg of next row.

Work one row without shaping.

Cast (bind) off rem 16[18] sts.

RIGHT FRONT

Work as given for left front, reversing all shaping and foll chart between markers for right front.

SLEEVES (both alike)

Cast on 31[35] sts, using 5mm (US 8) needles and yarns Na.

Work 21 rows in K1, P1 rib as given for back.

Next row (inc) (WS) Using yarns Za, P1, (M1, P2) 15[17] times. (46[52] sts)

Change to 6mm (US 10) needles and work 76 rows in patt from chart for sleeve, and AT THE SAME TIME shape sides of sleeve by inc one st at each end of 3rd row and every foll alt row until there are 70[76] sts, then at each end of every foll 3rd

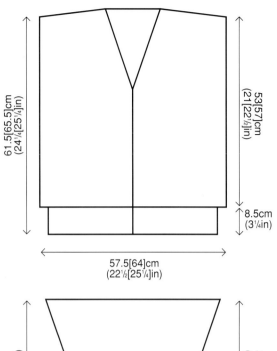

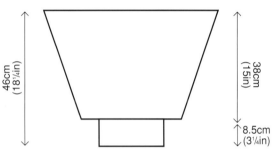

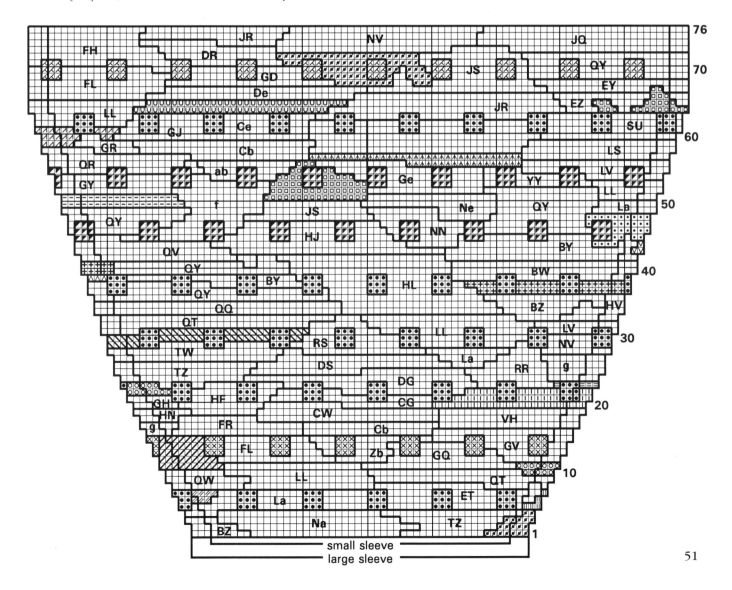

row until there are 96[102] sts, taking extra sts
into patt as they occur.
Cast (bind) off loosely and evenly.

POCKET EDGINGS (both alike)
Press all pieces gently on WS, using a warm iron
over a damp cloth and avoiding ribbing.
With RS facing, using 5mm (US 8) needles and
yarn g, pick up and K25 sts evenly between
markers on side edge of front.
K one row (WS) to form foldline.
Work 4 rows in st st, beg with a K row.
Cast (bind) off loosely and evenly.

POCKET LININGS
With RS facing, using 5½mm (US 9) needles and
yarn g, pick up and K25 sts evenly between
markers on left side edge of back and work in st
st, beg with a P row, and AT THE SAME TIME cast on 8
sts at beg of first row and dec one st at end of 5th
row and every foll alt row until 20 sts rem.
Cast (bind) off evenly.
Work right pocket lining as given for left pocket
lining, reversing all shaping.

BUTTONHOLE BAND
With RS facing, using 5mm (US 8) needles and
yarns YT, pick up and K58[63] sts evenly along
right front edge for a woman's jacket or left front
edge for a man's, leaving shaped neck edge
unworked.
Next row (buttonhole) (WS) P3, *cast (bind) off
2 sts, P8[9] including st already on needle after
cast (bind) off,* rep from * to * 4 times more,
cast (bind) off 2 sts, P3.
Next row Knit across row, casting on 2 sts to
replace those cast (bound) off on previous row.
P one row.
Change to yarn g and K 2 rows to form foldline.
Work 8 rows more in st st, beg with a K row, and
AT THE SAME TIME work buttonholes on rows 2 and
3 to correspond with those already made.
Cast (bind) off loosely and evenly.

BUTTON BAND
Work the button band on the other front as given
for the buttonhole band, but omitting the
buttonholes.

COLLAR
Cast on 153 sts, using 5mm (US 8) needles and
yarns YE.
Cont in K1, P1 rib in colour sequence outlined
below, and AT THE SAME TIME shape collar by casting
(binding) off 3 sts at beg of row 10 and every foll
row until 75 sts rem.
Colour sequence: one row ET, one row HR, row
FR, one row FL, one row LL, one row La, one row
Na, one row DR, one row DY, one row CY, 2 rows
Cb, one row Zb, one row JR, one row RQ, one
row QY, one row QW, one row WB, 2 rows BZ,
one row JR, one row LV, 2 rows Le, one row g, 2
rows Na, one row HS, one row NV, one row VG,
one row Ge, one row Ne, one row NN and 2
rows NZ.
Cast (bind) off firmly, using yarns NZ.

FINISHING
Use backstitch for all seams on main knitting and
an edge to edge st for ribbing.
Join both shoulder seams.
Fold front bands to WS along foldline and slip
stitch loosely in place.
Attach shaped edge of collar neatly to neckline,
with centre back of cast (bound) off row at centre
back neck and cast on edge of collar and foldlines
of front bands in one continuous line.
Place markers 30[32]cm (12[12¾]in) down from
shoulder seam on back and fronts.
Set in sleeve between markers.
Join sleeve seams and side seams above and
below pockets.
Fold pocket edgings to WS along foldline and slip
stitch loosely in place.
Slip stitch pocket linings loosely to WS of fronts.
Sew on buttons to correspond with buttonholes.
Press seams.

TAPESTRY LEAF

I was asked to design a knitted garment to go with a wonderful Liberty fabric. Having long admired the style and mood of that old London store, I jumped at the chance. I took a leaf from a darkish colourway of one of their current designs and enlarged it into my overlapping Tapestry Leaf jacket. Knitted in Kid Silk and wool, it has a luxurious feel and drape.

SIZE AND MEASUREMENTS
One size to fit up to 122cm (48in) bust
Finished measurement at underarm 138cm (54½in)
Length from shoulder 70.5cm (27¾in)
Sleeve length 36cm (14¼in)

YARN
Rowan Kid Silk – 25g (1oz) balls, Lambswool Tweed – 50g (1¾oz) balls, Donegal Lambswool Tweed –25g (1oz) hanks, Lightweight DK – 25g (1oz) hanks, and Designer DK – 50g (1¾oz) balls

			Shade no	Amount
A	Kid Silk	Coal	999	12 balls
B	Kid Silk	Goat	994	3 balls
C	Kid Silk	Garnet	992	3 balls
D	Kid Silk	Holly	990	2 balls
E	Kid Silk	Steel Blue	991	1 ball
F	Kid Silk	Smoke	998	2 balls
G	Kid Silk	Silver Blonde	995	1 ball
H	Kid Silk	Pot-pourri	996	1 ball
J	Kid Silk	Old Gold	989	2 balls
L	Kid Silk	Violet	982	1 ball
N	Kid Silk	Crushed Berry	993	2 balls
Q	Don Twd	Wine Berry	181	2 balls
R	Lbs Twd	Heliotrope	186	1 ball
S	Ltwt DK		407	4 hanks
T	Des DK		663	1 ball
U	Ltwt DK		151	2 balls
V	Des DK		652	1 ball
W	Des DK		660	1 ball
Y	Don Twd	Roseberry	480	1 hank
Y	Don Twd	Cinnamon	479	1 hank

Note: Yarn Y is one strand of 480 and one strand of 479 used together.
Yarns are shown on the charts either by their relevant letters or by symbols. Refer to the chart key for symbols.

NEEDLES AND BUTTONS
Pair of 3mm (UK no 11) (US 3) needles
Pair of 3¾mm (UK no 9) (US 5) needles
Seven buttons

TENSION/GAUGE
22 sts and 27 rows to 10cm (4in) measured over patterned st st using 3¾mm (US 5) needles.

The large simple leaves of the Tapestry Leaf jacket were inspired by a Liberty print.

Check your tension (gauge) carefully before beginning and change needle size if necessary.

NOTES
The pattern is comprised of a series of interlocking leaves. Use separate lengths of yarn (the intarsia method) for the leaves, linking one colour to the next by twisting them around each other where they meet on WS to avoid holes. Carry yarn A, used for veining and outlining certain areas of colour, loosely across the back of every row, weaving in every 3 or 4 sts (the fairisle method).

Read charts from right to left for K (RS odd-numbered) rows and from left to right for P (WS even-numbered) rows unless otherwise stated.

BACK
Cast on 140 sts, using 3mm (US 3) needles and yarn U.
Work 35 rows in K1, P1 rib in the foll colour sequence:
2 rows U, 4 rows B, one row Q, one row R, 3 rows Q, 2 rows C, 2 rows U, one row C, one row T, 2 rows R, 2 rows B, 3 rows S, one row B, one row A, 4 rows Q, one row V, one row U, one row R and 2 rows A.
Next row (inc) (WS) Using yarn A, rib 4, (pick up horizontal loop before next st and work into back of it — called *make one* or *M1* —, rib 12) 11 times, M1, rib 4. (152 sts)
Change to 3¾mm (US 5) needles and cont in patt from chart (see Notes) for back which is worked entirely in st st, beg with a K row.
Work 158 rows in patt, marking each end of rows 18 and 55 with coloured thread for pocket openings and row 81 for sleeve position, so ending with a WS row.
Shape back neck
Chart row 159 Work 67 sts in patt, cast (bind) off centre 18 sts, work in patt to end.

Chart row 160 Work in patt to neck edge, then turn and leave rem sts on a st holder.
Work each side of neck separately, foll chart throughout.
Cast (bind) off 8 sts at beg of next row.
Leave rem 59 sts on a st holder.
With WS facing, rejoin yarn to rem sts, cast (bind) off 8 sts, work in patt to end.
Work one row without shaping.
Leave rem 59 sts on a st holder.

LEFT FRONT

Cast on 70 sts, using 3mm (US 3) needles and yarn U.
Work 35 rows in K1, P1 rib as given for back.
Next row (inc) (WS) Using yarn A, rib 5, (M1, rib 12) 5 times, M1, rib 5. (76 sts)
Change to 3¾mm (US 5) needles and work 139 rows in patt from chart between markers for left front, marking positions of pocket opening and sleeve on side edge as for back, so ending with a RS row.
Shape front neck
Foll chart throughout, cast (bind) off at beg of next row and foll alt rows, 7 sts once, 3 sts once, 2 sts once and one st 5 times.
Work without shaping until chart row 161 has been completed.
Leave rem 59 sts on a st holder.

RIGHT FRONT

Work as given for left front, reversing all shaping and foll chart between markers for right front.

SLEEVES (both alike)

The sleeve is picked up between the sleeve markers and knitted down to the cuff. Should a longer sleeve be required this can be achieved by knitting more rows after the last dec row.
Press back and fronts gently on WS, using a warm iron over a damp cloth and avoiding ribbing.
Join shoulder seams by grafting sts together, using yarn R.
Pick up for sleeve
With RS facing, using 3¾mm (US 5) needles and yarn A, pick up and K132 sts evenly between sleeve markers.
Work in patt from chart between markers for sleeve, beg with row 1 at left hand side of chart with a P row and working through to row 77, AT THE SAME TIME shape sides by dec one st at each end of 12th row and every foll 3rd row until there are 116 sts, then every foll alt row until there are 80 sts, then every foll 3rd row until there are 76 sts, taking extra sts into patt as they occur and working extra rows after chart row 77 if a longer sleeve is desired, ending with a WS row.
Change to 3mm (US 3) needles.
Next row (dec) (RS) Using yarn U, K3, (K2tog, K2) 17 times, K2tog, K3. (58 sts)
Work 27 rows in K1, P1 rib in the foll colour sequence:
3 rows A, one row R, one row U, one row V, 4 rows Q, one row A, one row B, 3 rows S, 2 rows B, 2 rows R, one row T, one row C, 2 rows U, 2 rows C and 2 rows Q.
Cast (bind) off evenly in rib, using yarn Q.

POCKET EDGINGS (both alike)

With RS facing, using 3mm (US 3) needles and yarn A, pick up and K34 sts evenly between markers on side edge of front.
K one row (WS) to form foldline.
Work 7 rows in st st, beg with a K row.
Cast (bind) off loosely and evenly.

POCKET LININGS

With RS facing, using 3¾mm (US 5) needles and yarn A, pick up and K34 sts evenly between markers on left side edge of back and work in st st, beg with a P row, and AT THE SAME TIME cast on 8 sts at beg of first row and dec one st at beg of 2nd row and every foll alt row until 19 sts rem.
Cast (bind) off evenly.
Work right pocket lining as given for left pocket lining, reversing all shaping.

BUTTONHOLE BAND

With RS facing, using 3mm (US 3) needles and yarn A, pick up and K134 sts evenly along right front edge.
Next row (WS) Purl, using yarn A.
Next row (buttonhole) (RS) Using yarn U, K3, *cast (bind) off 2 sts, K19 including st already on needle after cast (bind) off,* rep from * to * 5 times more, cast (bind) off 2 sts, K3.
Next row Using yarn U, purl across row, casting on 2 sts to replace those cast (bound) off on previous row.
Using yarn Q, K 2 rows to form foldline.
Next row Knit, using yarn D.
Next row Purl, using yarn A and making buttonholes to correspond with those already made.
Next row Using yarn A, knit across row, casting on 2 sts to replace those cast (bound) off on previous row.
Work 7 rows in st st in the foil colour sequence:
2 rows A, 3 rows U, one row Q and one row A.
Cast (bind) off loosely and evenly, using yarn A.

BUTTON BAND

Work on other front as given for right front band, omitting buttonholes.

The richly coloured Tapestry Leaf jacket has proved one of my most popular designs ever.

* See yarns in instructions for explanation of colour Y

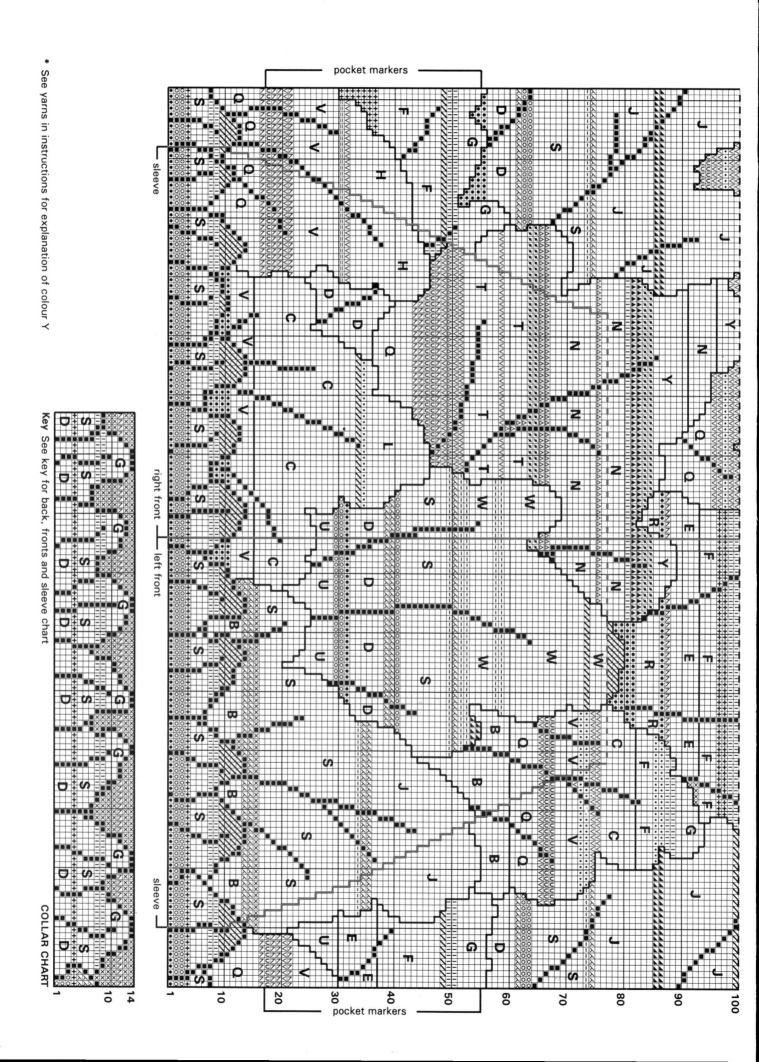

Key See key for back, fronts and sleeve chart

COLLAR CHART

COLLAR

Fold front bands to WS along foldline and slip stitch loosely in place.

With RS facing, using 3¾mm (US 5) needles and yarn A, pick up and K31 sts evenly up right front neck, 35 sts across back neck and 31 sts down left front neck. (97 sts)

Work 14 rows in patt from chart for collar which is worked entirely in st st, beg at left hand side of chart with a P row.

Change to 3mm (US 3) needles and P 2 rows, using yarn Q.

Then work 19 rows in st st, beg with a P row in the foll colour sequence:

One row D, 4 rows A, 2 rows B, 3 rows U, one row Q, 2 rows A, one row B, one row R, one row U and 3 rows A.

Cast (bind) off loosely and evenly, using yarn A.

FINISHING

Use backstitch for all seams on main knitting and an edge to edge st for ribbing.

Press sleeves gently on WS, using a warm iron over a damp cloth and avoiding ribbing.

Fold collar to WS along foldline and slip stitch loosely in place.

Press collar lightly with a warm iron over a damp cloth, stretching slightly along its length.

Join sleeve and side seams above and below pockets.

Fold pocket edgings to WS along foldline and slip stitch loosely in place.

Slip stitch pocket linings loosely to WS of fronts.

Sew on buttons to correspond with buttonholes.

Press seams.

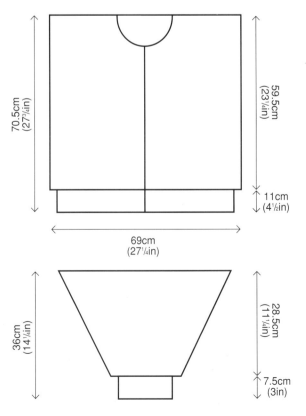

70.5cm (27¾in)
59.5cm (23¼in)
11cm (4½in)
69cm (27¼in)
36cm (14¼in)
28.5cm (11¼in)
7.5cm (3in)

AFGHAN

I've always loved playing with scales of geometric patterns, and squares are the easiest to knit of them all. Influences spring from Moroccan carpets and aerial views of farmlands. When finished, it reminded me of crocheted afghans I'd seen as a child – hence the name. The chunky wools on this promise quick knitting. Rowan's magazine Number Ten has a cardigan version of this pattern that may suit some people better – I could see it as a long coat as well, similar to the Windows coat on pages 36 and 37. I hope you feel inspired to do some really bright over-the-top colourways of your own on this pattern. Since it bears comparison to an afghan, why not do a large one with a diagonal striped border, like the Tumbling Blocks bedcover on page 63?

SIZE AND MEASUREMENTS

One size to fit up to 112cm (44in) bust/chest
Finished measurement at underarm 136cm (53½in)
Length from shoulder 69cm (27¼in)
Sleeve length 43.5cm (17¼in)

YARN

Rowan Magpie – 100g (3½oz) hanks, Lambswool Tweed – 50g (1¾oz) balls, Designer DK – 50g (1¾oz) balls, Fox Tweed DK – 50g (1¾oz) hanks, Donegal Lambswool Tweed – 25g (1oz) hanks, and Kid Silk – 25g (1oz) balls

			Shade no	Amount
A	Des DK		639	3 balls
B	Magpie	Raven	62	1 hank
C	Magpie	Neptune	612	1 hank
D	Magpie	Ginger	505	1 hank
E	Magpie	Blueberry	119	1 hank
F	Magpie	Cocoa	607	1 hank
G	Magpie	Sealord	608	1 hank
H	Magpie	Comanche	503	1 hank
J	Don Twd	Bay	485	3 hanks
K	Lbs Twd	Heliotrope	186	2 balls
L	Don Twd	Bramble	484	2 hanks
M	Lbs Twd	Khol	185	1 ball
N	Fox Twd	Hare	853	1 hank
P	Don Twd	Leaf	481	3 hanks
Q	Kid Silk	Crushed Bry	993	3 balls
R	Kid Silk	Garnet	992	2 balls
T	Kid Silk	Old Gold	989	3 balls
U	Kid Silk	Steel Blue	991	1 ball
W	Kid Silk	Pot Pourri	996	2 balls
Y	Kid Silk	Smoke	998	1 ball
Z	Magpie		763	1 hank

Note: The finer yarns are used in combination, e.g. AA means use 2 stands of yarn A, NT means use one strand of yarn N and one strand of yarn T, PPP means use 3 strands of yarn P. Yarns are shown on the chart either by their relevant letters or by symbols. Refer to the chart key for symbols.

Needles

Pair of (UK no 6) (US 8) needles
Pair of 6mm (UK no 4) (US 10) needles

TENSION GAUGE

15 sts and 22 rows to 10 cm (4 in) measured over patterned st st using 6mm (US 10) needles. *Check your tension (gauge) carefully before beginning and change needle size if necessary.*

NOTES

When working the colourwork pattern, use the intarsia method, using a separate length of yarn for each area of contrasting colour and linking one colour to the next by twisting them around each other where they meet on WS to avoid holes.
Read chart from right to left for K (RS odd-numbered) rows and from left to right for P (WS even-numbered) rows.

BACK

Cast on 90 sts, using 5mm (US 8) needles and yarn C.
Work 17 rows in K1, P1 rib in the foll colour sequence:
One row JJ, one row QQ, one H, 2 rows KK, one row F, 2 rows E, one row TT, one row D, 2 rows PPP, 2 rows Z, one row QW, one row WW and one row G.
Next row (inc) (WS) Using yarn G, P1, (pick up horizontal loop before next st and purl into back of it — called *make one purlwise or M1p —, P8) 11 times, Pl. (102 sts)
Change to 6mm (US 10) needles and cont in patt from chart (see Notes) for back which is worked entirely in st st, beg with a K row.**
Work 134 rows in patt.
Cast (bind) off loosely and evenly.

FRONT

Work as given for back to **.
Work 114 rows in patt from chart for front, so ending with a WS row.
Shape front neck
Chart row 115 (RS) Work 47 sts in patt, then turn and leave rem sts on a st holder.
Work each side of neck separately, foll chart throughout.
Cast (bind) off 3 sts at beg of next row.
Dec one st at neck edge on next 8 rows. (36 sts)

The Afghan crewneck, when finished, reminded me of crocheted afghans.

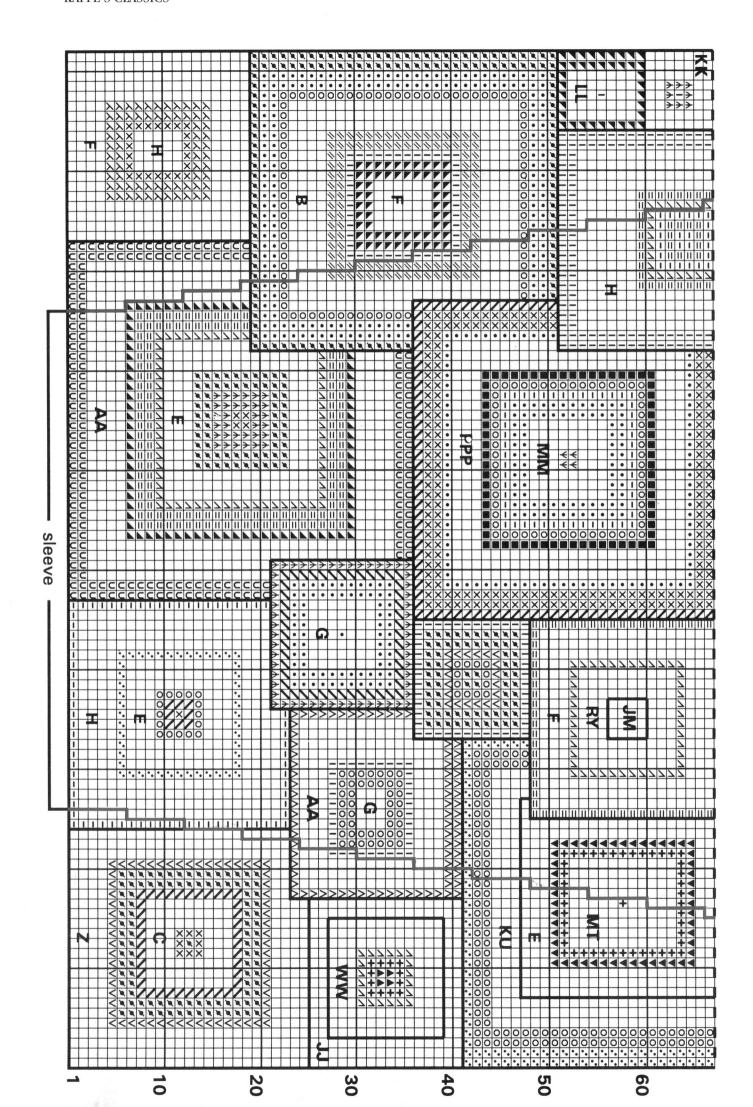

sleeve

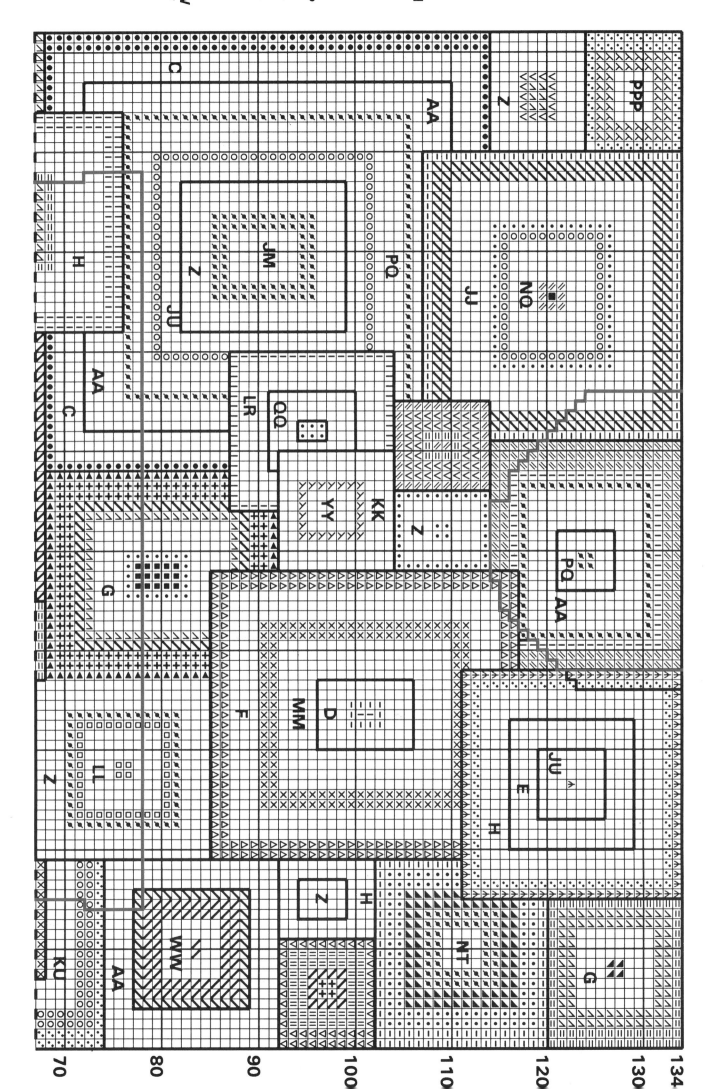

Key
● AA
▨ AY
■ B
• C
⊡ D
⊠ E
▽ F
⊟ G
+ H
↘ JJ
⊞ KK
◩ KR
◪ KU
◹ LL
⊟ LM
◪ LQ
◪ MM
■ MP
◪ NN
◺ NP
◹ NQ
⊡ NR
▾ NT
◣ PPP
△ PT
□ PW
∴ QQ
▲ QY
◪ RR
≡ TT
△ TY
◁ WW
▽ WY
▽ YY
◹ Z

70　　80　　90　　100　　110　　120　　130　　134

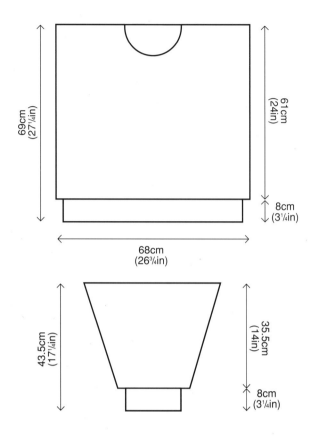

*The Afghan crewneck, pictured at
Kentwell Hall, Suffolk.*

Cont without shaping until front matches back to
shoulder, ending with a WS row.
Cast (bind) off loosely and evenly.
With RS facing, rejoin yarn to rem sts, cast (bind)
off centre 8 sts, work in patt to end.
Work one row without shaping.
Complete to match first side of neck, reversing all
shaping.

SLEEVES (both alike)
Cast on 44 sts, using 5mm (US 8) needles and
yarn C.
Work 17 rows in K1, P1 rib in colour sequence as
given for back.
Next row (inc) (WS) Using yarn G, P2, (M1p, P8)
5 times, M1p, P2. (50 sts)
Change to 6mm (US 10) needles and work 78
rows in patt from chart between markers for
sleeve, and AT THE SAME TIME shape sides by inc
one st at each end of 7th row and every foll 6th
row until there are 74 sts, taking extra sts into

patt as they occur.
Cast (bind) off loosely and evenly.

NECKBAND
Press all pieces gently on WS, using a warm iron
over a damp cloth and avoiding ribbing.
Join right shoulder seam, using backstitch.
With RS facing, using 5mm (US 8) needles and
yarn F, pick up and K23 sts evenly down left front
neck, 8 sts across centre front, 23 sts up right
front neck and 30 sts across back neck. (84 sts)
Work 5 rows in K1, P1 rib in the foll colour
sequence:
2 rows KK, row H, one row QQ and one row JJ.
Cast (bind) off evenly in rib, using yarn C.

FINISHING
Use backstitch for all seams on main knitting and
an edge to edge st for ribbing.
Join left shoulder seam and neck band.
Place markers 24.5cm (9¾in) down from shoulder
seam on back and front.
Set in sleeves between markers.
Join side and sleeve seams. Press seams.

TUMBLING BLOCKS

When I was casting about for a pattern to knit on a large bedcover, the tumbling blocks and diagonal stripes were naturals for the job: easy to knit, rhythmical patterns that more or less knit themselves once you get going. Using double yarns means it grows quickly and makes interesting shadings of colour. I'm sure you all have stores of yarns that beg to be put into a project like this one – I look forward to seeing new colourways.

MEASUREMENTS

Finished bedcover measures 226cm (89in) by 236cm (93in). Centre panel measures 128cm (50in) by 168cm (66in).

YARN

Rowanspun Tweed – 100g (3½oz) hanks, Rowan Designer DK – 50g (½oz) balls, Lambswool Tweed – 50g (½oz) balls, Botany – 25g (1oz) hanks, Magpie – 100g (3½oz) hanks, Lightweight DK – 25g (1oz) hanks, Donegal Lambswool Tweed – 25g (1oz) hanks, and Chunky Fox Tweed – 100g (3½oz) hanks

			Shade no	Amount
E	Rwnspn	Caper	762	1 hank
F	Rwnspn	Ember	763	1 hank
G	Des DK		662	2 balls
H	Des DK		659	2 balls
K	Des DK		671	2 balls
L	Des DK		658	1 ball
M	Ltwt DK		407	2 hanks
N	Botany		118	3 hanks
O	Des DK		681	1 ball
P	Des DK		682	2 balls
R	Lbs Twd	Dark Ore	183	1 ball
S	Botany		100	1 hank
T	Magpie	Cloud	507	1 hank
U	Magpie	Sealord	608	1 hank
V	Magpie	Pumice	301	1 hank
W	Ltwt DK		93	2 hanks
X	Ltwt DK		45	2 hanks
Y	Ltwt DK		127	6 hanks
Z	Ltwt DK		69	3 hanks
a	Ltwt DK		106	3 hanks
b	Ltwt DK		134	2 hanks
d	Ltwt DK		51	4 hanks
e	Ltwt DK		53	2 hanks
f	Ltwt DK		100	2 hanks
g	Ltwt DK		56	3 hanks
h	Don Twd	Leaf	481	3 hanks
j	Don Twd	Marram	472	2 hanks
k	Don Twd	Mist	466	2 hanks
l	Don Twd	Rye	474	3 hanks
m	Don Twd	Cinnamon	479	4 hanks
n	Don Twd	Bay	485	2 hanks

Above and overleaf *The Tumbling Blocks bedcover spills from the window of the medieval Kentwell Hall. I am wearing the Blue Diamond cotton crewneck.*

p	Don Twd	Sapphire	486	2 hanks
q	Don Twd	Elderberry	490	5 hanks
r	Don Twd	Bramble	484	4 hanks
s	Don Twd	Juniper	482	1 hank
t	Don Twd	Bark	475	4 hanks
w	Don Twd	Shale	467	4 hanks
y	Don Twd	Pepper	473	1 hank
2	Ch Fox	Moorland	871	1 hank
3	Ch Fox	Loch	872	1 hank
4	Magpie	Admiral	504	2 hanks

Note: The finer yarns are used in combination, e.g. SSe means use 2 strands of yarn S and one strand of yarn e, Wd means use one strand of yarn W and one strand of yarn d.
Yarns are shown on the charts either by their relevant letters or by symbols.

NEEDLES

Pair of 5½mm (UK no 5) (US 9) needles
Pair of 4½mm (UK no 7) (US 7) needles

TENSION/GAUGE

14 sts and 20 rows to 10cm (4in) measured over patterned st st using 5½mm (US 9) needles.
Check your tension (gauge) carefully before beginning and change needle size if necessary.

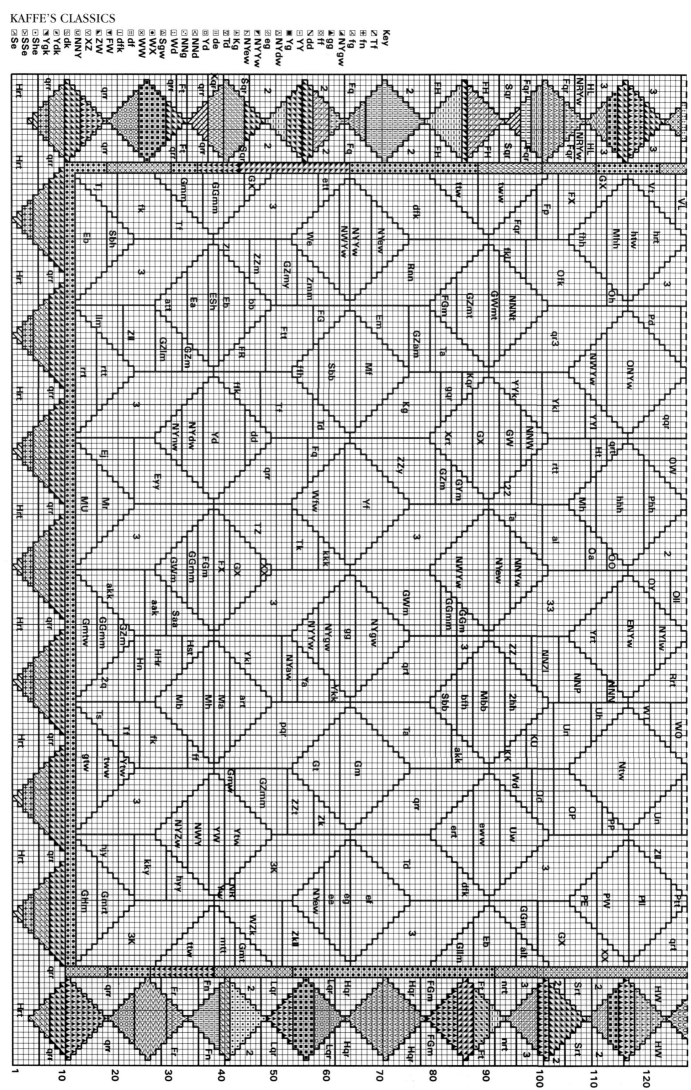

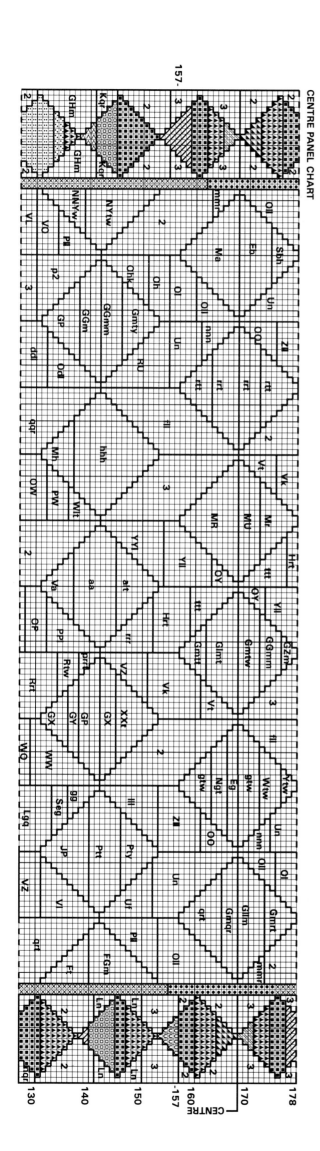

CENTRE PANEL CHART

NOTES

When working the colourwork pattern, use the intarsia method, using a separate length of yarn for each area of contrasting colour and linking one colour to the next by twisting them around each other where they meet on WS to avoid holes.

Read charts from right to left for K (RS odd-numbered) rows and from left to right for P (WS even-numbered) rows unless otherwise stated.

CENTRE PANEL

Cast on 180 sts, using 5½mm (US 9) needles and yarn 2.

Work in patt from chart (see Notes) for centre panel which is worked entirely in st st, beg with a K row.

Work 178 rows in patt.

Now to complete second half of centre panel TURN CHART UP SIDE DOWN and work back through chart to row one, starting at row 157.

Cast (bind) off loosely and evenly.

BORDER SECTION ONE (make 2)

Cast on 159 sts, using 5½mm (US 9) needles and yarn 4.

Work in patt from chart for border which is worked entirely in st st, beg with a K row.

Work 69 rows in patt, so ending with a RS row.

Chart row 70 (WS) Cast (bind) off 91 sts, work in patt to end. (68 sts)

Cont from chart until all 237 rows have been completed.

Cast (bind) off.

BORDER SECTION TWO (make 2)

Cast on 159 sts, using 5½mm (US 9) needles and yarn 4.

Work 69 rows in patt from chart for border, *but beg chart row one at right hand side of chart with a purl row*, thus reversing the corner.

Chart row 70 (RS) Cast (bind) off 91 sts, work in patt to end. (68 sts)

Cont from chart until all 237 rows have been completed.

Cast (bind) off.

FINISHING

Press all pieces gently on WS, using a warm iron over a damp cloth.

Hems

With RS facing, using 4½mm (US 7) needles and one strand each of yarns 4 and q, pick up and K159 sts along bottom edge of one border section one.

Next row (WS) Knit (to form foldline).

Next row K2tog, K to end.

Next row P to last 2 sts, P2tog.

Rep last two rows 5 times more.

Cast (bind) off loosely and evenly.

With RS facing, using 4½mm (US 7) needles and one strand each of yarns 4 and q, pick up and K166 sts up side edge of same border section.

Next row (WS) Knit.

Next row K to last 2 sts, K2tog.

Next row P2tog, P to end.

Rep last two rows 5 times more.

Cast (bind) off loosely and evenly.

Complete other border section one in the same way.

Work hems on border sections two as for section one, reversing shaping.

Sew the four border sections together to form a large rectangle.

Sew centre panel in place.

Slip stitch hems in place on WS.

Press hems and seams.

BORDER CHART

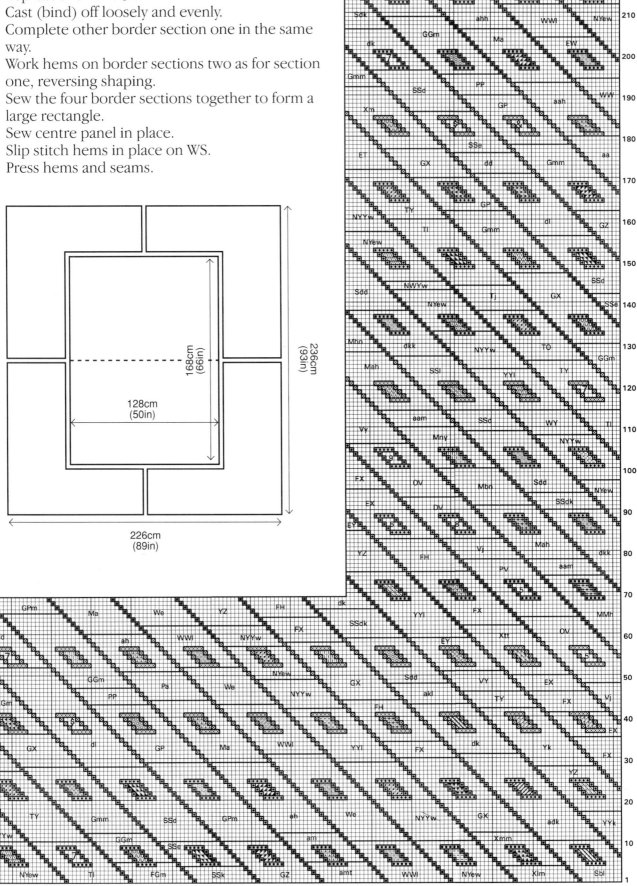

BROCADE

Classic brocades have always attracted me, wildly flowery, leafy and ribbony with the restraint of two very close colour tones. Here I've used the French conceit of running a brilliant shot of colour through the deep gold of the background. The shape is designed to be comfortable on larger ladies and wonderfully drapey on broomsticks. Because it is worked with only two colours in a row it is one of my easiest designs to knit, once you get over the bother of working from a graph. When I first started publishing patterns, I encountered a resistance to knitting graphs, as most British knitters were brought up on line-by-line written instructions. One knitter actually took the graph for this Brocade sweater and wrote it out as 'two cream, six yellow, one cream, four yellow, etc.' That one graph must have taken up pages! Nowadays, most knitters know that covering up the top of the knitting graph with card or a ruler, so that the line to be worked is at the top of one's view, makes it easier to follow.

The Brocade crewneck, a simple two colour a row knit made from cuff to cuff in one piece.

SIZE AND MEASUREMENTS
One size to fit up to 112cm (44in) bust
Finished measurement at underarm 130cm (51½in)
Length from shoulder 72cm (28¼in)
Sleeve length 42cm (16½in)

YARN
Rowan Lightweight DK – 25g (1oz) hanks and Fine Cotton Chenille – 50g (1¾oz) balls

			Shade no	Amount
A	Ltwt DK		30	15 hanks
B	Fine Chen	Gorse	391	12 balls
C	Ltwt DK		410	2 hanks
D	Ltwt DK		121	1 hank
E	Ltwt DK		110	1 hank
F	Ltwt DK		424	1 hank
G	Ltwt DK		36	1 hank
H	Ltwt DK		33	2 hanks
J	Ltwt DK		63	1 hank
L	Ltwt DK		22	1 hank

Note: Yarns are shown on the chart by symbols. Refer to the chart key table for symbols.

NEEDLES
Pair of 3¾mm (UK no 9) (US 5) needles
Pair of 4½mm (UK no 7) (US 7) needles
Circular needle 4½mm (UK no 7) (US 7) 100cm (40in) long
Circular needle 3¾mm (UK no 9) (US 5) 40cm (16in) long for neckband

TENSION/GAUGE
22 sts and 26 rows to 10cm (4in) measured over patterned st st using 4½mm (US 7) needles. *Check your tension (gauge) carefully before beginning and change needle size if necessary.*

NOTES
The chart shows half of the right sleeve and half of the front. The left hand side of the sleeve is a mirror image of the right hand side (and the back a mirror image of the front), so when the centre is reached on each row, the chart is read in reverse to complete the row.

When working the colourwork pattern, use the fairisle method (2 colours in a row), carrying the colour not in use loosely across back of work, weaving in every 3 or 4 sts and spreading sts to their correct width to keep them elastic. Read chart from right to left (to centre – see above) for K (RS odd-numbered rows and from left to right for P (WS even-numbered) rows unless otherwise stated.

BACK, FRONT AND SLEEVES (one piece)
Beg at lower edge (cuff edge) of right sleeve, cast on 62 sts, using 3¾mm (US 5) needles and yarn L.

these 10 sts, then work in patt across 147 sts of back. (300 sts)

Work 59 rows without shaping, so ending with a WS row.

Shape sides of front and back

Next row (RS) Using yarn B, K across first 90 sts, then turn and leave rem sts on a spare needle. Cast (bind) off these 90 sts for left side edge of front.

With RS facing, rejoin yarn to rem sts, work centre 120 sts in patt, then with yarn B, K rem 90 sts.

Using yarn B, cast (bind) off 90 sts at beg of next row for left side of back, working rem 120 sts in patt. (120 sts)

Change to same size ordinary needles.

Work 3 rows without shaping on these sts for for left sleeve.

Shape left sleeve

Dec one st at each end of next row and every foll 4th row until there are 78 sts.

Work one row without shaping, so ending with chart row 1 (WS).

Change to 3¾mm (US 5) needles and work dec row as foll:

Next row (dec) (RS) Using yarn B, *K2tog, K3, rep from * to last 3 sts, K2tog, K1. (62 sts)

Work 25 rows in K1, P1 rib, reversing colour sequence given for first cuff.

Cast (bind) off evenly in rib, using yarn L.

NECKBAND

Press piece gently on WS, using a warm iron over a damp cloth and avoiding ribbing.

With RS facing, using short 3¾mm (US 5) circular needle and yarn B, beg at centre back neck and pick up and K130 sts evenly all around neck edge.

Work 6 rounds (RS always facing) in K1, P1 rib in the foll colour sequence:

One round B, 2 rounds A, 2 rounds B, and one round D.

Cast (bind) off loosely in rib, using yarn D.

FINISHING

Join side and sleeve seams, carefully matching the patt and using backstitch for seam on main knitting and an edge to edge st for ribbing.

Lower ribbing

With RS facing, using long 3¾mm (US 5) circular needle and yarn B, beg at one side seam and pick up and K300 sts evenly all around lower edge of back and front.

Work 14 rounds (RS always facing) in K1, P1 rib in the foll colour sequence:

One round B, (2 rounds A, 2 rounds B) 3 times, and one round D.

Cast (bind) off loosely in rib, using yarn D.

Press seams.

The rich golds, shot through with brilliant colours, of the Brocade crewneck, shimmer in winter sunshine.

MOSAIC

This is so called because I first saw this design on an ancient mosaic from Ravenna in Italy. As I was writing this book a letter arrived from a fan showing this design reworked as a crewneck sweater – very handsome it is too! With all the patterns in this book, do approach them as interchangeable ideas – if you want a certain jacket as a waistcoat or the other way round, feel free to adapt the ideas. I always get a great thrill seeing these new uses of my designs.

SIZE AND MEASUREMENTS

One size to fit up to 102cm (40in) bust/chest
Finished measurement at underarm 112cm (44in)
Length from shoulder 52.5cm (20¾in)

YARN

Rowan Donegal Lambswool Tweed – 25g (1oz) hanks

			Shade no	Amount
A	Don Twd	Black	491	4 hanks
B	Don Twd	Mist	466	3 hanks
C	Don Twd	Pepper	473	2 hanks
D	Don Twd	Sapphire	486	2 hanks
E	Don Twd	Roseberry	480	2 hanks
F	Don Twd	Juniper	482	2 hanks
G	Don Twd	Cinnamon	479	2 hanks
H	Don Twd	Leaf	481	1 hank
J	Don Twd	Tarragon	477	2 hanks
L	Don Twd	Bark	475	2 hanks

Note: Yarns are shown on the chart either by their relevant letters or by symbols. Refer to the chart key for symbols.

NEEDLES AND BUTTONS

Pair of 3mm (UK no 11) (US 2) needles
Pair of 3¼mm (UK no 10) (US 3) needles
Circular needle 3mm (UK no 11) (US 2) 100cm (40in) long
Circular needle 3¼mm (UK no 10) (US 3) 100cm (40in) long
Five buttons

TENSION/GAUGE

26 sts and 38 rows to 10cm (4in) measured over patterned st st using 3¼mm (US 3) needles.
Check your tension (gauge) carefully before beginning and change needle size if necessary.

NOTES

When working the colourwork pattern, use the intarsia method, using a separate length of yarn for each area of contrasting colour and linking one colour to the next by twisting them around each other where they meet on WS to avoid holes. Read chart from right to left for K (RS odd-numbered) rows and from left to right for P (WS even-numbered) rows.

BACK

Cast on 146 sts, using 3mm (US 2) needles and yarn A.
** For hem work 9 rows in st st, beg with a K row, so ending with a K row.
Next row (WS) Knit (to form foldline). **
Change to 3¼mm (US 3) needles and cont in patt from chart (see Notes) for back which is worked entirely in st st, beg with a K row.
Work 112 rows in patt, so ending with a WS row.
Shape armholes
Foll chart throughout, cast (bind) off 8 sts at beg of next 2 rows.
Dec one st at each end of next row and every foll alt row until 112 sts rem.
Work without shaping until chart row 200 has been completed, so ending with a WS row.
Shape shoulders
Cast (bind) off 11 sts at beg of next 4 rows and 12 sts at beg of foll 2 rows.
Cast (bind) off rem 44 sts for back neck.

LEFT FRONT

Cast on 73 sts, using 3mm (US 2) needles and yarn A.
Work as given for back from ** to **.
Change to 3¼mm (US 3) needles and work 104 rows in patt from chart between markers for left front, so ending with a WS row.
Shape front neck and armhole
Foll chart throughout, dec one st at end (neck edge) of next row and every foll 4th row 12 times in all, then at same edge on every foll 5th row until 34 sts rem, and AT THE SAME TIME when front matches back to armhole ending with a WS row, shape armhole as given for back.
Work without shaping until front matches back to shoulder, ending with a WS row.
Shape shoulder
Cast (bind) off 11 sts at beg of next row and foll alt row.
Work one row without shaping.
Cast (bind) off rem 12 sts.

RIGHT FRONT

Work as given for left front, reversing all shaping and foll chart between markers for right front.

The Mosaic waistcoat (right) was inspired by an ancient mosaic in Ravenna, and looks stunning here with just a casual shirt whose earthy colour tones perfectly. It is shown here with the Lattice crewneck (page 78).

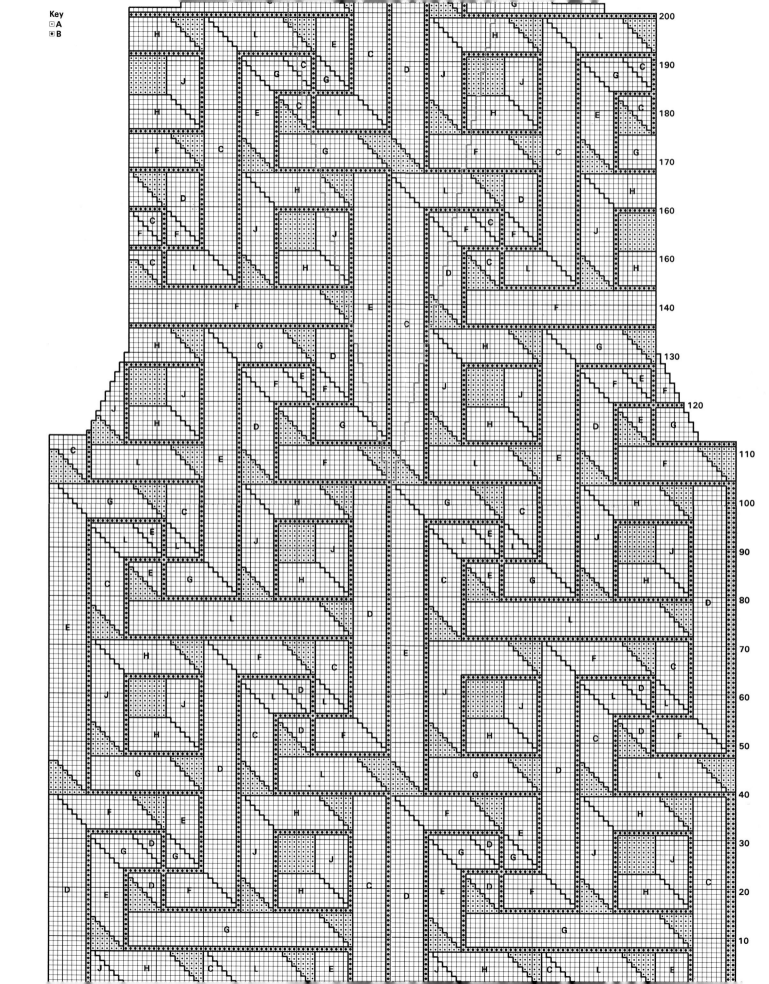

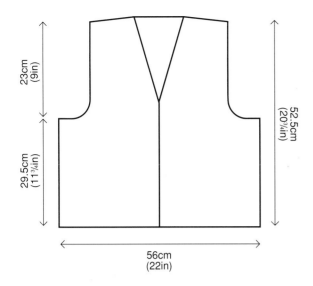

23cm
(9in)

29.5cm
(11¾in)

52.5cm
(20¾in)

56cm
(22in)

FRONT BANDS (worked in one piece)
Press all pieces gently on WS, using a warm iron over a damp cloth.
Join both shoulder seams, using backstitch.
With RS facing, using 3¼mm (US 3) circular needle and yarn D, beg at foldline on right front and pick up and K80 sts evenly up right front edge to beg of neck shaping, 81 sts up right neck edge to shoulder seam, one st at shoulder seam, 45 sts across centre back, one st at shoulder seam, 81 sts down left front neck edge to beg of neck shaping and 80 sts down left front edge to foldline. (369 sts)
Working back and forth in rows (not rounds), cont as foll:
Next row (WS) (P3 in yarn D, P3 in yarn E) to last 3 sts, P3 in yarn D.
Man's version only:
Next row (buttonhole) (RS) Keeping stripes as set on previous row, K to last 79 sts, *cast (bind) off 2 sts, K16 including st already on needle after cast (bind) off,* rep from * to * 3 times more, cast (bind) off 2 sts, K to end.

Woman's version only:
Next row (buttonholes) (RS) Keeping stripes as set on previous row, K7, *cast (bind) off 2 sts, K16 including st already on needle after cast (bind) off,* rep from * to * 3 times more, cast (bind) of 2 sts, K to end.
Both versions:
Next row (WS) Keeping colours as set, purl across row, casting on 2 sts to replace those cast (bound) off on previous row.
Next row Knit, using yarn F.
Next row Knit, using yarn F (to form foldline).
Change to 3mm (US 2) circular needle and yarn A and work 6 rows in st st, beg with a K row, and AT THE SAME TIME work buttonholes on rows 2 and 3 to correspond with those already made.
Cast (bind) off evenly.

ARMBANDS (both alike)
With RS facing, using 3¼mm (US 3) needles and yarn A, pick up and K144 sts evenly around armhole edge.
K one row (WS) to form foldline.
Change to 3mm (US 2) needles and work 4 rows in st st, beg with a K row.
Cast (bind) off evenly.

FINISHING
Join side seams and armbands, using backstitch.
Fold hem along lower edge to WS along foldline and slip stitch loosely into place.
Fold front bands and neckband in half to WS along foldline and slip stitch loosely in place.
Fold armhole facings to WS along foldline and slip stitch loosely into place.
Using yarn A, neatly sew bottom of front bands and facings together.
Sew on buttons to correspond with buttonholes.
Press seams.

LATTICE

It was good to have handsome manly colours in cotton instead of the usual pastels. I like wearing this all year round. The inspiration is from Islamic tiles: the little diamonds at each crossover of the lattice were originally small stars. You could make them stars again to add a little extra finesse if you like.

SIZE AND MEASUREMENTS

One size to fit up to 102cm (40in) bust/chest
Finished measurement at underarm 118cm (46½in)
Length from shoulder 58cm (23in)
Sleeve length 49cm (19½in)

YARN

Rowan Cotton Glacé – 50g (1¾oz) balls,
Wool/Cotton – 40g (1½oz) balls, and Nice Cotton – 50g (1¾oz) balls

			Shade no	Amount
A	Glacé	Provence	744	1 ball
B	Glacé	Gentian	743	1 ball
C	Glacé	Dijon	739	1 ball
D	Glacé	Granite	734	2 balls
E	Glacé	Black	727	1ball
F	Glacé	Matador	742	1 ball
G	Glacé	Rowan	736	2 balls
H	W/Cott	Sage	912	1 ball
J	W/Cott	Kashmir	910	1 ball
K	W/Cott	Musk	913	1 ball
L	W/Cott	Mandala	927	5 balls
M	W/Cott	Hibiscus	925	1 ball
O	W/Cott	Chocolate	921	1 ball
P	Nice	Rio	431	1 ball
R	Nice	Samba	435	2 balls
S	Nice	Adobe	434	2 balls
T	Nice	Fiesta	437	2 balls
U	Nice	Mardi-Gras	436	2 balls
V	Nice	Parade	430	1 ball

Note: Yarns are shown on the chart either by their relevant letters or by symbols.

NEEDLES

Pair of 2¾mm (UK no 12) (US 2) needles
Pair of 3¼mm (UK no 10) (US 3) needles

TENSION/GAUGE

25 sts and 34 rows to 10cm (4in) measured over patterned st st using 3¼mm (US 3) needles
Check your tension (gauge) carefully before beginning and change needle size if necessary.

NOTES

When working the colourwork pattern, use the intarsia method, using a separate length of yarn

The olive tones of the Lattice crewneck are set off well against the mossy barn.

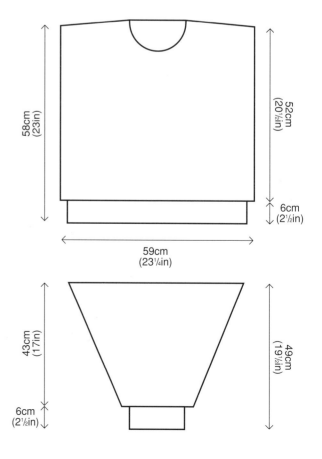

for each area of contrasting colour and linking one colour to the next by twisting them around each other where they meet on WS to avoid holes.
Read chart from right to left for K (RS odd-numbered) rows and from left to right for P (WS even-numbered) rows.

BACK
Cast on 131 sts, using 2¾mm (US 2) needles and yarn U.
Work 21 rows in K1, P1 rib in the foll colour sequence:
One row U, 3 rows S, 2 rows T, one row M, 3 rows G, 2 rows R, one row S, 2 rows E, one row R, 2 rows T, one row D, one row U and one row M.
Next row (inc) (WS) Using yarn M, rib 5, (pick up horizontal loop before next st and work into back of it — called *make one* or *M1* —, rib 8) 15 times, M1, rib 6. (147 sts)
Change to 3¼mm (US 3) needles and cont in patt from chart (see Notes) for back which is worked entirely in st st, beg with a K row. **
Work 176 rows in patt, marking each end of row 90 for position of sleeve, so ending with a WS row.
Shape shoulders
Foll chart throughout, cast (bind) off 17 sts at beg of next 6 rows.
Leave rem 45 sts on a st holder.

FRONT
Work as given for back to **.
Work 150 rows in patt from chart for front, marking each end of row 90 for position of sleeve, so ending with a WS row.
Shape front neck
Chart row 151 (RS) Work 66 sts in patt, then turn and leave rem sts on a st holder.
Work each side of neck separately, foll chart throughout.
Cast (bind) off 3 sts at beg of next row and foll 2 alt rows.
Dec one st at neck edge on next 6 rows. (51 sts)
Cont without shaping until front matches back to shoulder, ending with a WS row.
Shape shoulder
Cast (bind) off 17 sts at beg of next row and foll 2 alt rows.
With RS facing, return to rem sts, slip centre 15 sts onto a st holder, then rejoin yarn to rem sts, work in patt to end.
Work one row without shaping
Complete to match first side of neck, reversing all shaping.

SLEEVES (both alike)
Cast on 55 sts, using 2¾mm (US 2) needles and yarn U.

Work 21 rows in K1, P1 rib in colour sequence as given for back.
Next row (inc) (WS) Using yarn M, rib 7, (M1, rib 8) 6 times. (61 sts)
Change to 3¼mm (US 3) needles and work 146 rows in patt from chart between markers for sleeve, and AT THE SAME TIME shape sides by inc one st at each end of 3rd row and every foll 4th row until there are 133 sts, taking extra sts into patt as they occur.
Cast (bind) off evenly.

NECKBAND
Press all pieces gently on WS, using a warm iron over a damp cloth and avoiding ribbing.
Join right shoulder seam, using backstitch.
With RS facing, using 2¾mm (US 2) needles and yarn D, pick up and K32 sts evenly down left front neck, K15 sts from st holder, pick up and K32 sts up right front neck and K45 sts from st holder at back neck. (124 sts)
Work 8 rows in K1, P1 rib in the foll colour sequence:
2 rows D, 2 rows T, one row R, one row S and 2 rows G.
Cast (bind) off evenly in rib, using yarn M.

FINISHING
Use backstitch for all seams on main knitting and an edge to edge st for ribbing.
Join left shoulder seam and neckband.
Set in sleeves between markers.
Join side and sleeve seams.
Press seams.

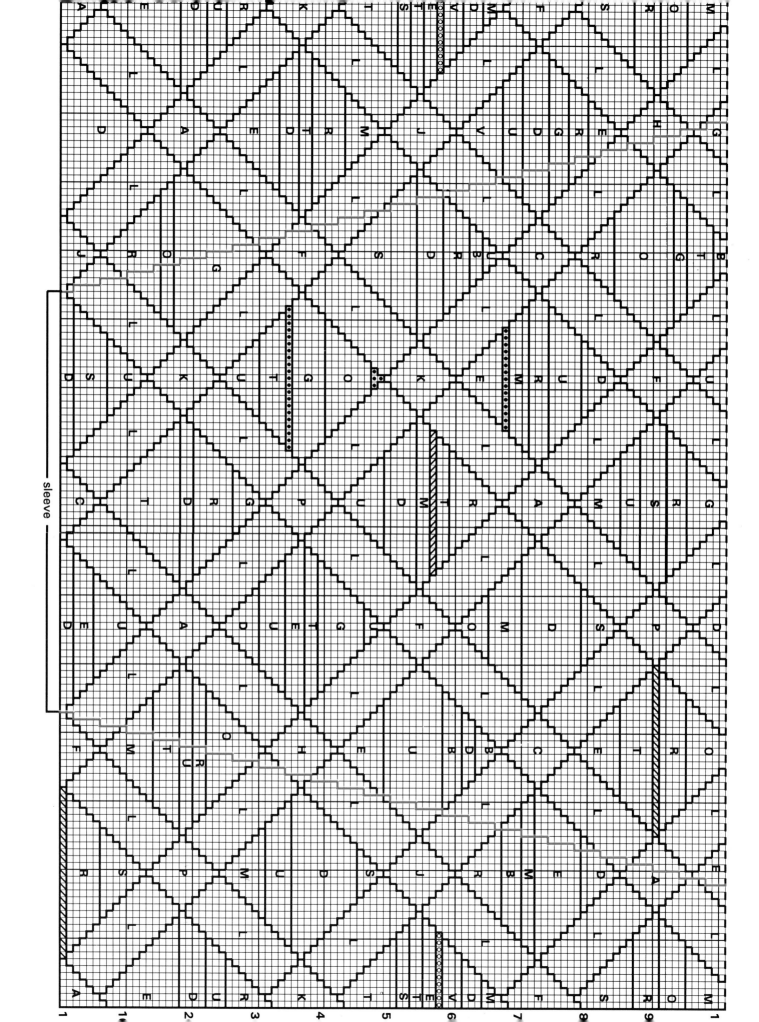

sleeve

Key ◨B ◩D ⊠G ◎T •U

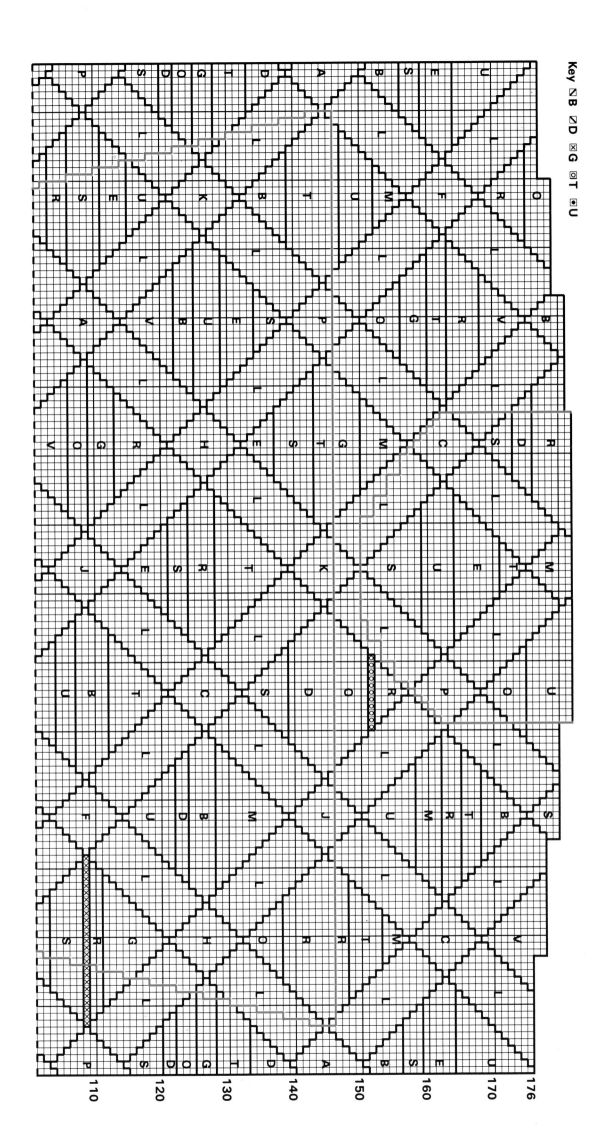

HERALDIC DOGS

I wanted a break from my densely packed repeats of geometric patterns and these leaping dogs seemed just the ticket. I found them in their flat outlined form in old textiles and pointed them out in *Glorious Inspiration*. At first I felt representational subject matter wasn't quite appropriate for knitting; that abstract pattern was more legitimate. With this self-imposed restraint, I viewed the world of decorative textiles and came to realise that often great patterns were made of objects or figures that formed delightfully rhythmic arrangements. These motifs were stylised and treated in a geometric fashion. This has led me to use houses, flowers, ribbons and now dogs with relish. The huge scale diagonal stripe put me in mind of heraldic shields so the name emerged. Here is a wool version, although the original was worked in double knitting cottons of similar tones.

SIZE AND MEASUREMENTS

One size to fit up to 107cm (42in) bust/chest
Finished measurement at underarm 124cm (49½in)
Length from shoulder 74cm (29¼in)
Sleeve length 48.5cm (19in)

YARN

Rowan Designer DK – 50g (1¾oz) balls and Lightweight DK – 25g (1oz) hanks

		Shade no	Amount
A	Des DK	663	4 balls
B	Des DK	625	6 balls
C	Des DK	672	2 balls
D	Des DK	685	2 balls
E	Des DK	616	1 ball
F	Des DK	662	2 balls
H	Des DK	671	1 ball
J	Des DK	652	2 balls
K	Des DK	70	1 ball
L	Ltwt DK	407	2 hanks

Note: Yarns are shown on the charts either by their relevant letters or by symbols. Refer to the chart key for symbols.

NEEDLES

Pair of 3¼mm (UK no 10) (US 3) needles
Pair of 4mm (UK no 8) (US 6) needles
Circular needle 3¼mm (UK no 10) (US 3) 40cm (16in) long

TENSION/GAUGE

21 sts and 25 rows to 10cm (4in) measured over patterned st st using 4mm (US 6) needles.

Check your tension (gauge) carefully before beginning and change needle size if necessary.

NOTES

When working the colourwork pattern, use the intarsia method, using a separate length of yarn for each area of contrasting colour and linking one colour to the next by twisting them around each other where they meet on WS to avoid holes.

Read charts from right to left for K (RS odd-numbered) rows and from left to right for P (WS even-numbered) rows unless otherwise stated.

BACK AND FRONT (one piece)

Beg at lower back edge, cast on 102 sts, using 3¼mm (US 3) needles and yarn B.
Work 21 rows in K1, P1 rib in the foll colour sequence:
One row B, 2 rows A, 2 rows J, 2 rows A, 2 rows J, 2 rows A, 2 rows B, 2 rows A, 2 rows J, 2 rows B and 2 rows A.
Next row (inc) (WS) Using yarn A, P4, (pick up horizontal loop before next st and purl into back of it — called *make one purlwise or M1p* —, P3, M1P, P4) 14 times. (130 sts)
Change to 4mm (US 6) needles and cont in patt from chart (see Notes) for back which is worked entirely in st st, beg with a K row.
Work 166 rows in patt, so ending with a WS row.
Divide for neck
Chart row 167 (RS) Work 50 sts in patt, then turn and leave rem sts on a st holder.
Work each side of neck separately, foll chart as foll:
Cast (bind) off 6 sts at beg of next row. (44 sts)
Work 2 rows without shaping.
Mark each end of last row (chart row 170) for shoulder line.
Work 10 rows more without shaping.
Shape front neck
Inc one st at neck edge on next row and 2 foll alt rows.
Work one row without shaping.
Cast on at end (neck edge) of next row and foll 2 alt rows, 2 sts once, 4 sts once and 5 sts once. (58 sts)
Work one row without shaping, so ending with chart row 192.
Leave these sts on a spare needle for right side front neck.
With RS facing, rejoin yarn to rem sts, cast (bind) off centre 30 sts, work in patt to end.
Work one row without shaping, then complete second side to match first side, reversing all shaping and ending with chart row 192.

The Heraldic Dogs crewneck, is knitted in richly-coloured deep tones appropriate to its medieval images.

back

back

A

B

A

G

10 20 30 40 50 60 70 80 90 100

1

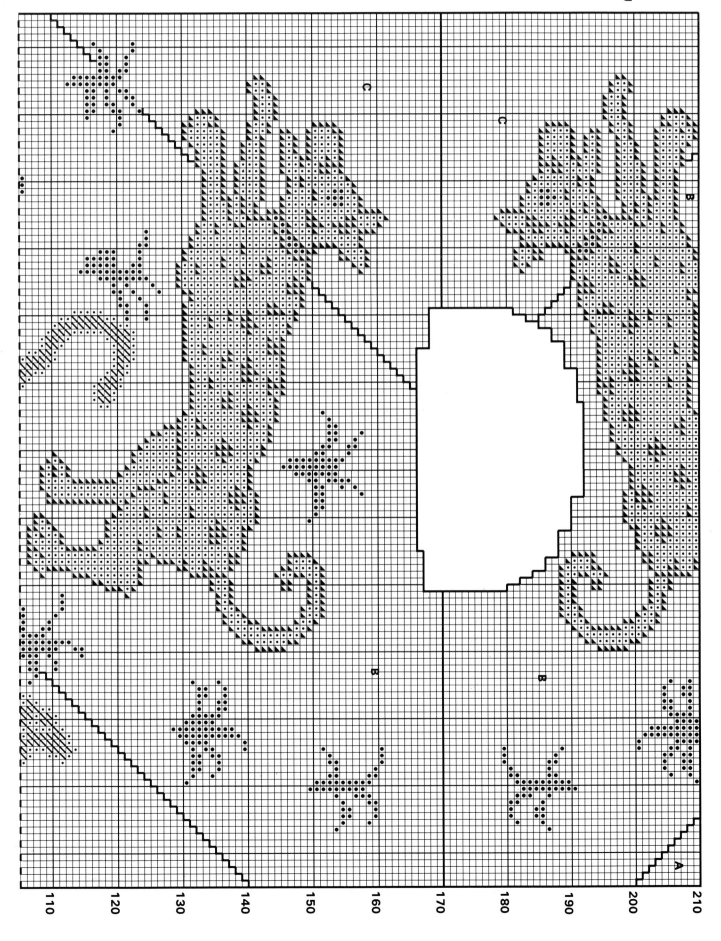

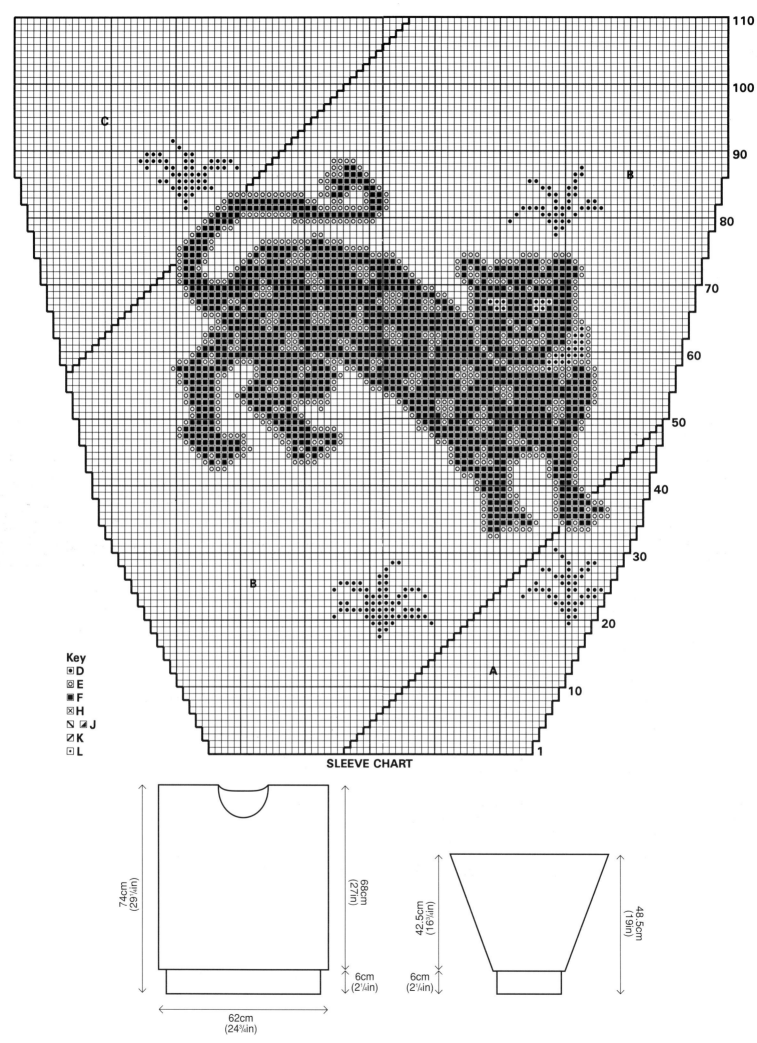

SLEEVE CHART

Key
- ⊡ D
- ⊙ E
- ■ F
- ⊠ H
- ◩ J
- ◪ K
- ⊡ L

74cm
(29¼in)

68cm
(27in)

6cm
(2¼in)

62cm
(24¾in)

42.5cm
(16¾in)

48.5cm
(19in)

6cm
(2¼in)

Leave sts on a spare needle for left side front neck.

Join right and left side

With RS facing, return to sts left on spare needle for right side front neck, rejoin yarn, work in patt across 58 sts, cast on 14 sts, work in patt across 58 sts left on spare needle for left side front neck. (130 sts)

Cont without shaping until chart row 210 has been completed, so ending with a WS row. Then complete the front by cont in patt from chart for back, beg at row 140 with a K row and working backwards through the rows (cont to read K rows from right to left and P rows from left to right), so ending at row 1 with a P row. Change to 3¼mm (US 3) needles and work dec row as foll:

Next row (dec) (RS) Using yarn A, K4, (K2tog, K2, K2tog, K3) 14 times. (102 sts)

Work 21 rows in K1, P1 rib, reversing colour sequence as given for back.

Rib one row in yarn B.

Cast (bind) off evenly in rib, using yarn B.

SLEEVES (both alike)

Cast on 42 sts, using 3¼mm (US 3) needles and yarn B.

Work 21 rows in K1, P1 rib in colour sequence as given for back.

Next row (inc) (WS) Using yarn A, P3, (M1p, P5) 7 times, M1p, P4. (50 sts)

Change to 4mm (US 6) needles and work 100 rows in patt from chart for sleeve, and AT THE SAME TIME shape sides by inc one st at each end of 3rd row and every foll alt row until there are 84 sts, then every foll 4th row until there are 110 sts, taking extra sts into patt as they occur.

Cont in patt from chart until sleeve measures 48.5cm (19in) from beg, ending with a WS row.

Cast (bind) off loosely and evenly.

NECKBAND

Press all pieces gently on WS, using a warm iron over a damp cloth and avoiding ribbing.

With RS facing, using 3¼mm (US 3) circular needle and yarn A, beg at left shoulder line and pick up and K23 sts evenly down left front neck, 14 sts across centre front, 23 sts up right front neck to shoulder line, 11 sts down right back neck, 30 sts across centre back and 11 sts up left

A close-up of the Heraldic Dogs crewneck, detailing the leaping dogs.

back neck. (112 sts)

Work 9 rounds (RS always facing) in K1, P1 rib in the foll colour sequence:

2 rounds A, 2 rounds B, 2 rounds J, 2 rounds A and one round B.

Cast (bind) off evenly in rib, using yarn B.

FINISHING

Use backstitch for all seams on main knitting and an edge to edge st for ribbing.

Place markers 27.5cm (11in) down from shoulder line on back and front.

Set in sleeves between markers.

Join side and sleeve seams. Press seams.

BIG CROSSES

This was first designed for an early Rowan book but was not very popular to begin with – the picture didn't show the pattern strongly enough. Yet over the years I have seen many good garments on satisfied customers so decided to include it here, recolouring it so it's practically a new design. It could be made with a very subtle tweedy palette if you saw fit; or could be exciting if knitted in wildly contrasting colours such as yellows and magentas.

SIZE AND MEASUREMENTS

One size to fit up to 122cm (48in) bust/chest
Finished measurement at underarm 154cm (61½in)
Length from shoulder 70cm (27½in)
Sleeve length 40cm (16in)

YARN

Rowan Magpie – 100g (3½oz) hanks, Lightweight DK – 25g (1oz) hanks, Chunky Fox Tweed – 100g (3½oz) hanks, Designer DK – 50g (1¾oz) balls, Kid Silk – 25g (1oz) balls, and Donegal Lambswool Tweed – 25g (1oz) hanks

			Shade no	Amount
A	Magpie	Shamrock	304	1 hank
B	Magpie	Woodland	300	1 hank
C	Ltwt DK		151	2 hanks
D	Magpie	Ivy	765	1 hank
E	Ch Fox	Charlie	875	2 hanks
F	Ch Fox	Biffo	876	2 hanks
G	Des DK		659	1 ball
H	Des DK		99	2 balls
K	Ltwt DK		52	2 hanks
L	Ltwt DK		106	2 hanks
M	Kid Silk	Steel	991	1 ball
N	Kid Silk	Garnett	992	3 balls
P	Kid Silk	Holly	990	1 ball
R	Don Twd	Bay	485	3 hanks
S	Don Twd	Cinnamon	479	1 hank
T	Don Twd	Roseberry	480	1 hank
V	Don Twd	Leaf	481	1 hank
W	Don Twd	Bramble	484	1 hank
X	Ltwt DK		38	2 hanks
Y	Don Twd	Elderberry	190	1 hank

Note: The finer yarns are used in combination, e.g. HH means use 2 strands of yarn H, BV means use one strand of yarn B and one strand of yarn V. Yarns are shown on the chart either by their relevant letters or by symbols.

NEEDLES AND BUTTONS

Pair of 4mm (UK no 8) (US 6) needles
Pair of 5mm (UK no 6) (US 8) needles
Pair of 6mm (UK no 4) (US 10) needles
Seven buttons

TENSION/GAUGE

14 sts and 20 rows to 10cm (4in) measured over patterned st st using 6mm (US 10) needles.
Check your tension (gauge) carefully before beginning and change needle size if necessary.

NOTES

When working the colourwork pattern, use the intarsia method, using a separate length of yarn for each area of contrasting colour and linking one colour to the next by twisting them around each other where they meet on WS to avoid holes.

Read chart from right to left for K (RS odd-numbered) rows and from left to right for P (WS even-numbered) rows.

BACK AND FRONTS (one piece)

Beg at lower edge of back, cast on 90 sts, using 5mm (US 8) needles and yarn F.
Work 13 rows in K1, P1 rib in the foll colour sequence:
One row F, 2 rows B, 3 rows PR, one row E, 3 rows HH, 2 rows KN and one row B.
Next row (inc) (WS) Using yarn B, rib 2, (pick up horizontal loop before next st and work into back of it — called *make one* or *M1* —, rib 5) 17 times, M1, rib 3. (108 sts)
Change to 6mm (US 10) needles and work in patt from chart (see Notes) for back which is worked entirely in st st, beg with a K row.
Work 124 rows in patt, marking each end of rows 9 and 43 for pocket openings, and 72nd row for position of sleeve, so ending with a WS row.
Divide for fronts
Chart row 125 (RS) Work 49 sts in patt, then turn leaving rem sts on a spare needle.
Work each front separately, foll chart throughout.
Shape right back neck
Cast (bind) off 5 sts at beg of next row. (44 sts)
Mark each end of last row for shoulder line.
Work one row without shaping.
Dec one st at beg of next row. (43 sts)
Work 7 rows without shaping, so ending at neck edge.
Shape front neck
Cast on 1 st at beg of next row and foll alt row, then 2 sts at beg of next 2 alt rows and 5 sts at beg of foll alt row. (54 sts).
Work without shaping until chart row 252 has

Back view of the Big Crosses jacket, knitted in vibrantly-coloured wools. A looser-knitted version than that shown here would create a softly-draped garment.

been completed, so ending with a WS row and marking position of sleeve and pocket opening as for back.

Change to 5mm (US 8) needles and continue with yarn B.

Next row (dec) (RS) K2, *K2tog, K4, rep from *, ending last rep K2 instead of K4. (45 sts)

Work 13 rows in K1, P1 rib, reversing colour sequence given for back and ending with 2 rows F instead of one.

Cast (bind) off evenly in rib, still using yarn F for cast off.

With RS facing, rejoin yarn to rem sts, cast (bind) off 10 sts, work in patt to end.

Work one row without shaping.

Mark each end of last row for shoulder line.

Cast (bind) off 5 sts at beg of next row and one st at beg of foll alt row. (43 sts)

Complete left front to match right front, reversing all shaping.

SLEEVES (both alike)

Cast on 32 sts, using 5mm (US 8) needles and yarn F.

Work 13 rows in K1, P1 rib in colour sequence as given for back.

Next row (inc) (WS) Using yarn B, rib 2, (M1, rib 3, M1, rib 2) 6 times. (44 sts)

Change to 6mm (US 10) needles and work 66 rows in patt from chart between markers for sleeve, and AT THE SAME TIME shape sides by inc one st at each end of 3rd row and inc one st at each end of every foll alt row until there are 72 sts, then inc one st at each end of every 4th row until there are 84 sts, taking extra sts into patt as they occur. Cast (bind) off loosely and evenly.

POCKET EDGINGS (both alike)

Press pieces gently on WS, using a warm iron and avoiding ribbing.

With RS facing, using 5mm (US 8) needles and

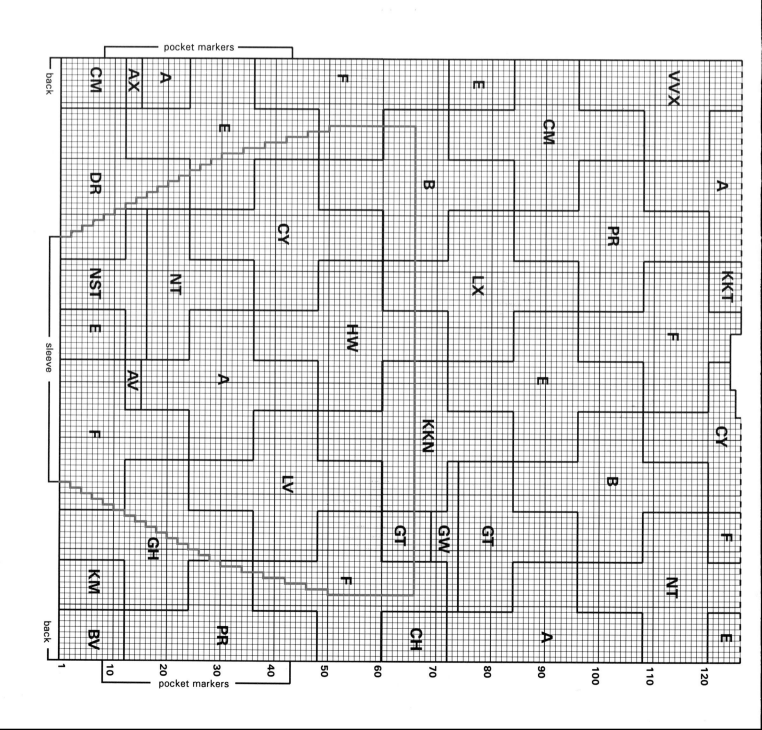

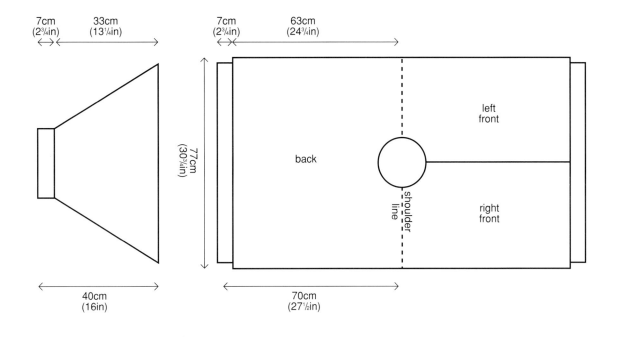

7cm
(2¾in)

33cm
(13¼in)

7cm
(2¾in)

63cm
(24¾in)

77cm
(30¾in)

40cm
(16in)

70cm
(27½in)

back

left
front

right
front

shoulder
line

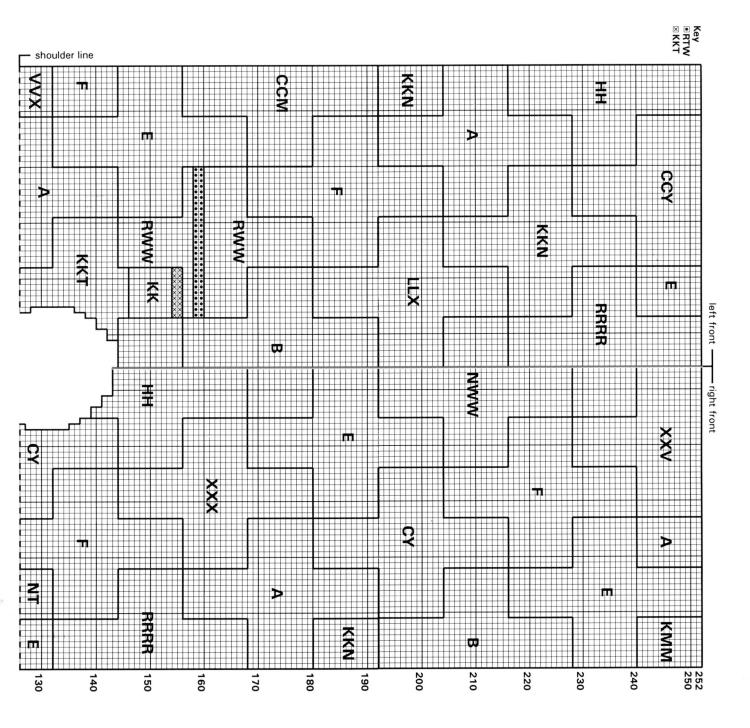

Key
⊡ RTW
⊠ KKT

shoulder line

VVX

F

CCM

KKN

HH

E

A

A

CCY

F

KKT

RWW

RWW

KKN

E

KK

LLX

RRRR

B

NWW

HH

E

XXV

CY

F

XXX

CY

F

A

F

A

NT

CY

E

E

RRRR

KKN

B

KMM

left front

right front

130 140 150 160 170 180 190 200 210 220 230 240 250
                                                              252

yarns DR, pick up and K26 sts evenly between pocket markers on side edge of front.
K one row (WS) to form foldline.
Work 4 rows in st st, beg with a K row.
Cast (bind) off loosely and evenly.

POCKET LININGS

With RS facing, using 6mm (US 8) needles and yarns DR, pick up and K26 sts evenly between pocket markers on left side edge of back and work in st st, beg with a P row, and AT THE SAME TIME cast on 4 sts at beg of first row and dec one st at beg of 2nd row and every foll K row until 17 sts rem.
Cast (bind) off evenly.
Work right pocket lining as given for left pocket lining, reversing all shaping.

BUTTON BAND

With RS facing, using 5mm (US 9) needles and yarns DR, pick up and K96 sts (12 sts from rib, 84 sts from main part) evenly along right front edge for a man's jacket or left front edge for a woman's.
P one row.
K 2 rows to form foldline.
Change to 4mm (US 6) needles and work 8 rows in st st, beg with a K row.
Cast (bind) off loosely.

BUTTONHOLE BAND

With RS facing, using 5mm needles and yarns DR, pick up and K96 sts as for button band along other front, and AT THE SAME TIME make buttonholes while picking up sts as foll:
Pick up and buttonhole row (RS) Pick up and K2 sts, *pick up and K2 sts, lift 2nd st on RH needle over first st and off needle, pick up and K one st,

lift 2nd st on RH needle over first st and off needle, pick up and K12 sts,* rep from * to * 6 times more, but ending last rep pick up and K one st.
Next row Purl across row, casting on 2 sts to replace those cast off on previous row.
K 2 rows to form foldline.
Change to 4mm (US 6) needles.
Next row (buttonhole) K2, * cast (bind) off 2 sts, K13 including st already on needle after cast (bind) off,* rep from * to * 5 times more, cast (bind) off 2 sts, K to end.
Next row Purl across row, casting on 2 sts to replace those cast (bound) off on previous row.
Work 6 rows st st, beg with a K row.
Cast (bind) off loosely.

COLLAR

Fold front bands to WS along foldline and slip stitch loosely in place.
With RS facing, using 5mm (US 9) needles and yarns DR, pick up and K68 sts evenly all around neck edge.
Work 13 rows in K1, P1 rib, reversing colour sequence given for back and ending with 2 rows of F instead of one.
Cast (bind) off evenly in rib, using yarn F.

FINISHING

Use backstitch for all seams on main knitting and an edge to edge st for ribbing.
Set in sleeves between markers.
Join sleeve seams and side seams above and below pockets.
Fold pocket edging to WS along foldline and slip stitch loosely in place.
Slip stitch pocket linings loosely to WS of fronts.
Sew on buttons to correspond with buttonholes.
Press seams.

Previous pages *The Big Cross jacket catching the soft sunlight of an English wood. I love the way the sharp greens of the cross are lifted by the mossy gate tones.*

BANDED TRIANGLE

I have a gorgeous black and white book of
Japanese brocade patterns including many
strong structures like this triangle pattern. As I
gaze at it, my mind fills in many different
colour combinations. My first version appeared
in contrasts of black, royal blue, beige and rust,
and didn't smoulder enough for my liking, so I
was glad of the chance to recolour it. These
mossy greens and grape bloom tones with
orange and navy borders really please me –
there is just enough tweed to give depth to
some of the larger areas. If you try your own
colours on this one, just make sure you include
light, medium and dark tones, creating
definition in your borders so that each colour
reads with clarity against its neighbouring
outline. This is one of those rhythmic patterns
that allows you to relax and knit, once you
have established each new row of triangles –
the first three rows where all the colours are
attached – and then it's simply a matter of
increasing or decreasing triangles one stitch
every other row. You needn't be a slave to your
graph until the next big colour change!

SIZE AND MEASUREMENTS
One size to fit up to 107cm (42in) bust/chest
Finished measurement at underarm 124cm (49in)
Length from shoulder 66cm (26in)
Sleeve length 41cm (16in)

YARN
Rowan Lightweight DK and Donegal Lambswool
Tweee – both 25g (1oz) hanks

			Shade no	Amount
A	Ltwt DK		620	2 hanks
B	Ltwt DK		501	3 hanks
C	Ltwt DK		71	3 hanks
D	Ltwt DK		70	3 hanks
E	Ltwt DK		97	3 hanks
F	Ltwt DK		54	3 hanks
G	Ltwt DK		11	2 hanks
H	Ltwt DK		52	1 hank
L	Ltwt DK		407	2 hanks
M	Ltwt DK		65	1 hank
N	Don Twd	Roseberry	480	2 hanks
P	Don Twd	Bark	475	2 hanks
R	Don Twd	Juniper	482	2 hanks
S	Don Twd	Leaf	481	2 hanks
T	Don Twd	Cinnamon	479	2 hanks
V	Don Twd	Storm	468	3 hanks
W	Ltwt DK		99	3 hanks
X	Ltwt DK		94	2 hanks

Note: The finer yarns are used in combination,
e.g. RR means use 2 strands of yarn R, NS means

*The Banded Triangle jacket is knitted in
mossy greens, tweeds and grape bloom
tones, and bordered with orange and
navy.*

use one strand of yarn N and one strand of yarn S.
Yarns are shown on the chart either by their
relevant letters or by symbols. Refer to the chart
key for symbols.

NEEDLES AND BUTTONS
Pair of 3¼mm (UK no 10) (US 3) needles
Pair of 4mm (UK no 8) (US 6) needles
Circular needle 3¼mm (UK no 10) (US 3) 100cm
(40in) long
Six buttons

TENSION/GAUGE
22 sts and 30 rows to 10cm (4in) measured over
patterned st st using 4mm (US 6) needles.
*Check your tension (gauge) carefully before
beginning and change needle size if necessary.*

NOTES
*When working the colourwork pattern, use the
intarsia method, using a separate length of yarn
for each area of contrasting colour and linking
one colour to the next by twisting them around
each other where they meet on WS to avoid holes.
Read chart from right to left for K (RS odd-*

numbered) rows and from left to right for P (WS even-numbered) rows.

BACK AND FRONTS (one piece)
Beg at lower back edge, cast on 137 sts, using 4mm (US 6) needles and yarn D.
Work in patt from chart for back which is worked entirely in st st, beg with a K row.
Work 170 rows in patt, marking each end of rows 12 and 50 for pocket openings, so ending with a WS row.

Divide for fronts
Chart row 171 (RS) Work 59 sts in patt, then turn and leave rem sts on a st holder.
Work each front separately, foll chart throughout.

Shape right back neck
Cast (bind) off 3 sts at beg of next row and foll alt row. (53 sts)

Shape front neck
Work 2 rows without shaping, then inc one st at neck edge on next row and every foll 6th row 4 times in all. (57 sts)
Work 5 rows without shaping, so ending with chart row 200 (WS).
Turn chart upside down, and reading even (K) rows from left to right and odd (P) rows from right to left, work down the chart from row 150 towards row 1.
Cont neck shaping by inc one st at neck edge on next row and every foll 6th row until there are 65 sts.
Work 5 rows without shaping.
Cast on 3 sts at neck edge on next row. (68 sts)
Work without shaping until chart row 1 has been completed, marking position of pocket opening on side edge as for back, so ending with a WS row.
Cast (bind) off loosely and evenly.
With RS facing, rejoin yarn to rem sts, cast (bind) off centre 19 sts, work in patt to end.
Complete left front to match right front, reversing all shaping.

SLEEVES (both alike)
Cast on 56 sts, using 3¼mm (US 3) needles and yarn F.
Work 26 rows in K2, P2 rib in the foll colour sequence:
2 rows each F and SS, 4 rows D, 2 rows each A and VV, 4 rows X, 2 rows each L, F, C, W and D.
Next row (inc) (WS) Using yarn D, rib 4, (pick up horizontal loop before next st and work into back of it — called *make one* or *M1* —, rib 2) 24 times, M1, rib 4. (81 sts)
Change to 4mm (US 6) needles and work 100 rows in patt from chart between markers for sleeves, and AT THE SAME TIME shape sides by inc one st at each end of every 3rd row until there are 95 sts, then every foll 4th row until there are 133 sts, taking extra sts into patt as they occur.
Cast (bind) off loosely and evenly.

POCKET EDGINGS (both alike)
Press all pieces gently on WS, using a warm iron over a damp cloth.
With RS facing, using 3¼mm (US 3) needles and yarn NN, pick up and K34 sts evenly between pocket markers on side edge of front.
K one row (WS) to form foldline.
Work 6 rows in st st, beg with a K row.
Cast (bind) off loosely and evenly.

POCKETS LININGS
With RS facing, using 4mm (US 6) needles and yarn NN, pick up and K34 sts between pocket markers on left side edge of back and work in st

The new tweedy version of the Banded Triangle jacket, looking distinctly at home in an English country house.

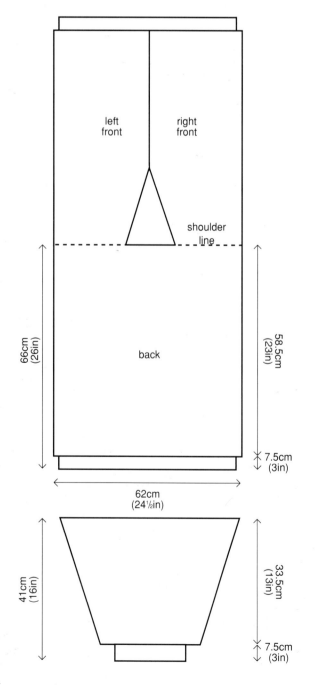

left
front

right
front

shoulder
line

66cm
(26in)

58.5cm
(23in)

back

7.5cm
(3in)

62cm
(24½in)

41cm
(16in)

33.5cm
(13in)

7.5cm
(3in)

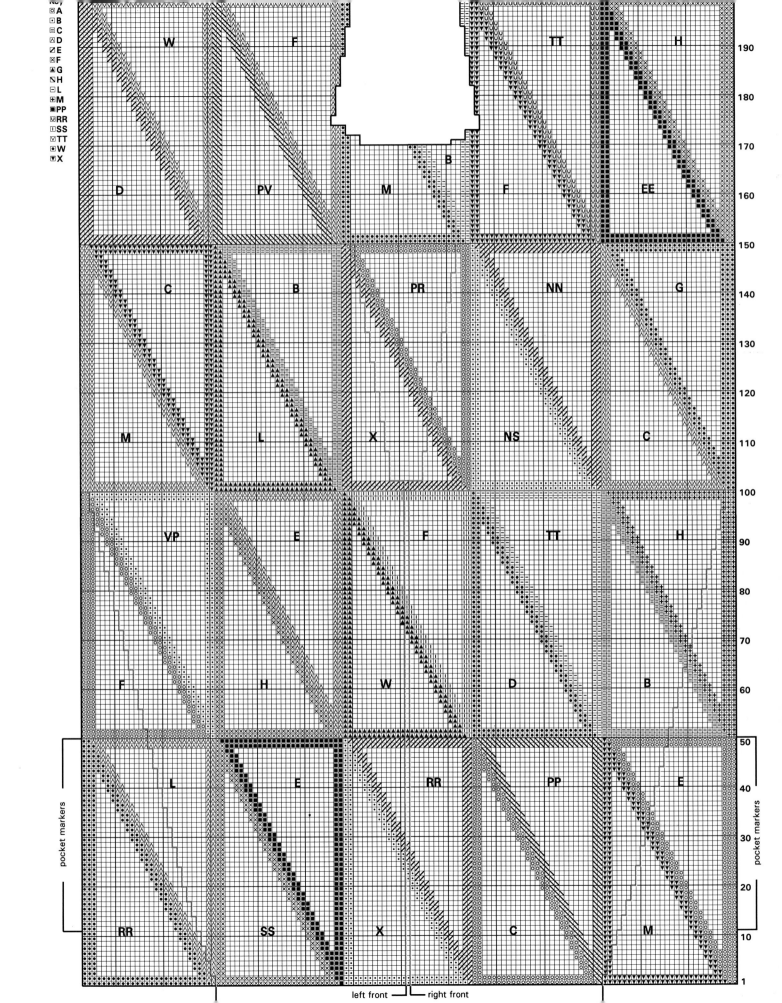

st, beg with a P row, and AT THE SAME TIME cast on 4 sts at beg of first row and dec one st at beg of 2nd row and every foll K row until 18 sts rem.
Cast (bind) off evenly.
Work right pocket lining as given for left pocket lining, reversing all shaping.

LOWER RIBBING
Place markers 30cm (11¾in) down from shoulder line on back and fronts.
Set in sleeves between markers, using backstitch. Join sleeve seams and side seams above and below pockets.
With RS facing, using 3¼mm (US 3) circular needle and yarn D, pick up and K67 sts evenly along lower left front edge, 134 sts across back and 67 sts along lower right front edge. (268 sts)
Work 26 rows in K1, P1 rib in the colour sequence given for cuff, but reversing order.
Work one more rib row in yarn F.
Cast (bind) off evenly in rib, using yarn F.

BUTTONHOLE BAND
With RS facing, using 3¼mm (US 3) needles and yarn VV, pick up and K88 sts evenly along right front edge for a woman's jacket or left front edge for a man's, leaving shaped neck edge unworked.
P one row. K one row.
Woman's version only:
Next row (buttonholes) (WS) P2, *cast (bind) off 2 sts, P16 including st already on needle after cast (bind) off,* rep from * to * 3 times more, cast (bind) off 2 sts, P8, cast (bind) off 2 sts, P2.
Man's version only:
Next row (buttonholes) (WS) P2, cast (bind) off 2 sts, P8 including st already on needle after cast (bind) off, *cast (bind) off 2 sts, P16,* rep from * to * 3 times more, cast (bind) off 2 sts, P2.

Both versions:
Next row Knit across row, casting on 2 sts to replace those cast (bound) off on previous row.
K 2 rows to form foldline.
Work 8 rows in st st, beg with a P row, and AT THE SAME TIME work buttonholes on rows 1 and 2 to correspond with those already made.
Cast (bind) off loosely and evenly.

BUTTON BAND
Work on other front as given for buttonhole band, omitting buttonholes.

COLLAR
Cast on 268 sts, using 3¼mm (US 3) circular needle and yarn F.
Working back and forth in rows, work 6 rows in K2, P2 rib in colour sequence given for sleeve cuffs.
Shape collar by casting (binding) off 4 sts at beg of next 24 rows and 6 sts at beg of next 12 rows, and AT THE SAME TIME cont in rib in colour sequence given for cuff, then after 26 rows have been completed from beg, work 4 rows more D, 3 rows VV, 2 rows B, 2 rows RR, and 5 rows E. (100 sts)
Cast (bind) off evenly in rib, using yarn E.

FINISHING
Fold front bands to WS along foldline and slip stitch loosely in place.
Attach shaped edge of collar to neck edge, fixing the straight row ends of collar to cast (bound) off sts at centre front.
Fold pocket edgings to WS along foldline and slip stitch loosely in place. Slip stitch pocket linings loosely to WS of fronts. Sew on buttons to correspond with buttonholes. Press seams.

LEOPARD SKIN

I was once brought a leopard pelt to knit from and was thrilled at all the colours I perceived in it. This is a long intense knit, being three colours a row in fine yarns, but the results are very satisfying according to those who have stayed the course. Doesn't our Norwegian model look a treat against those old priory walls!

SIZE AND MEASUREMENTS
One size to fit up to 112cm (44in) bust/chest
Finished measurement at underarm 131cm (51½in)
Length from shoulder 67cm (26½in)
Sleeve length 45.5cm (18in)

YARN
Rowan Donegal Lambswool Tweed, Lightweight DK, Kid Silk and Botany – all 25g (1oz) hanks/balls, and Designer DK – 50g (1¾oz) balls

			Shade no	Amount
A	Don Twd	Dolphin	478	2 hanks
B	Kid Silk	Silver Blond	995	3 balls
C	Des DK		680	3 balls
D	Don Twd	Pepper	473	3 hanks
E	Don Twd	Bramble	484	2 hanks
F	Ltwt DK		86	5 hanks
G	Ltwt DK		10	1 hank
H	Ltwt DK		5	3 hanks
J	Ltwt DK		64	2 hanks
L	Ltwt DK		4	1 hank
N	Ltwt DK		104	1 hank
Q	Ltwt Dk		652	3 hanks
R	Kid Silk	Potpourri	996	2 balls
S	Ltwt DK		422	3 hanks
T	Don Twd	Mist	466	3 hanks
U	Ltwt DK		8	3 hanks
V	Don Twd	Pickle	483	3 hanks
W	Ltwt DK		604	3 hanks
Y	Botany		118	2 hanks

Note: Use yarn single except for back and front ribbing, cuffs, front bands and neck band where yarn should be used doubled.
Yarns are shown on the chart by symbols. Refer to the colour sequence table for symbols.

NEEDLES AND BUTTONS
Pair of 3mm (UK no 11) (US 3) needles
Pair of 3¾mm (UK no 9) (US 5) needles
Circular needle 3mm (UK no 11) (US 3) 100cm (40in) long
Eight buttons

TENSION/GAUGE
30 sts and 28 rows to 10cm (4in) measured over patterned st st using 3¾mm (US 5) needles.

Check your tension (gauge) carefully before beginning and change needle size if necessary.

NOTES
When working the colourwork pattern, use the fairisle method (3 colours a row), carrying the 2 colours not in use loosely across back of work, weaving in every 3 or 4 sts and spreading sts to their correct width to keep them elastic.
Read chart from right to left for K (RS odd-numbered) rows and from left to right for P (WS even-numbered) rows.

BACK AND FRONTS (one piece)
Beg at lower edge of back, cast on 119 sts, using 3mm (US 3) needles and 2 strands of yarn A.
Using 2 strands of each yarn, work 21 rows in K1, P1 rib in the foll colour sequence:
2 rows B, one row C, 2 rows F, one row E, 2 rows S, one row B, 2 rows D, 2 rows T, 3 rows B, one row T, 2 rows U, one row F and one row D.
Next row (inc) (WS) Using 2 strands of yarn V, rib 2, pick up horizontal loop before next stitch and work into back of it — called *make one* or *M1* —, (rib 1, M1, rib 2, M1) 38 times, rib 1, M1, rib 2. (197 sts)
Change to 3¾mm (US 5) needles and (using only one strand of each yarn throughout) work in patt from chart (see Notes) for back which is worked entirely in st st, beg with a K row.
Work 160 rows in patt, marking each end of row 96 for position of sleeve, so ending with a WS row.
Shape neck and divide for fronts
Chart row 161 (RS) Work 78 sts in patt, cast (bind) off 41 centre sts, work in patt to end.
Chart row 162 Work in patt to neck edge, then turn and leave rem sts on a st holder.
Work each side of neck separately, foll chart throughout.
Cast (bind) off 7 sts at beg (neck edge) of next row and 4 sts at beg of foll alt row. (67 sts)
Work one row without shaping.
Mark each end of last row (chart row 166) for shoulder line.
Cont on these sts only for left front, working backwards through chart from shoulder line (completion of neck shaping is shown in full) and AT THE SAME TIME reversing order of colour sequence chart.
Work 5 rows without shaping.
** Inc one st at end (neck edge) of next row and 6 foll alt rows.
Work one row without shaping.

The Leopard Skin jacket with its three colours a row throughout, knitted in fine yarn, is a challenge to knit, but look at the results, shown to great effect against these textured monastery walls.

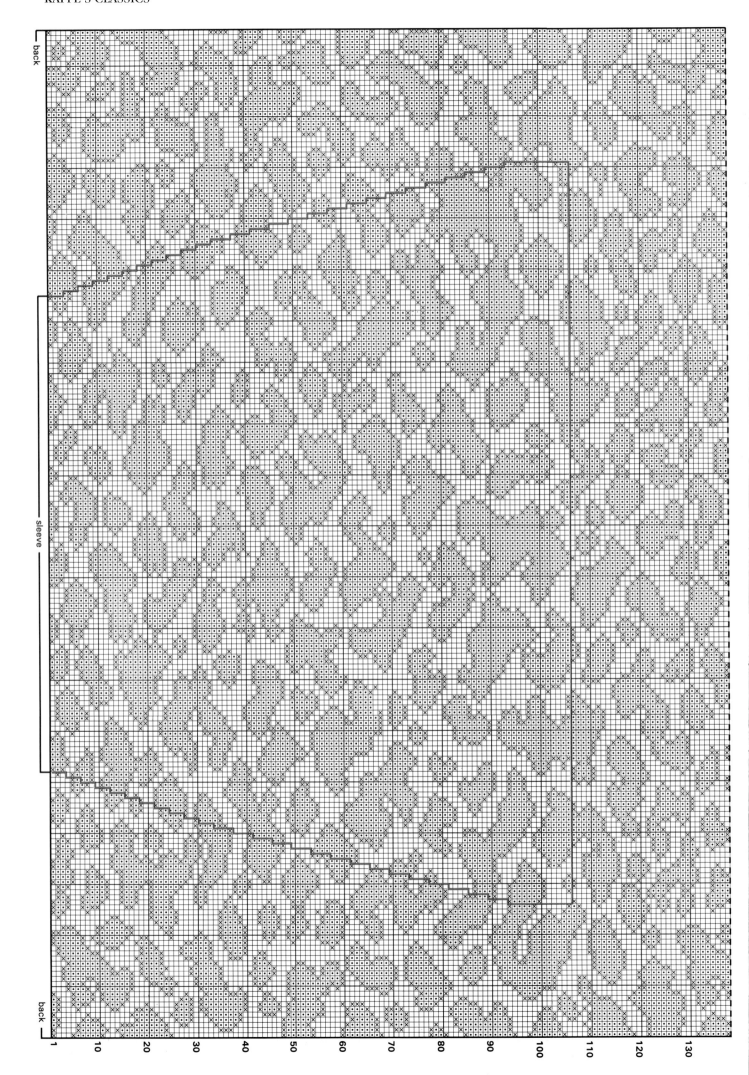

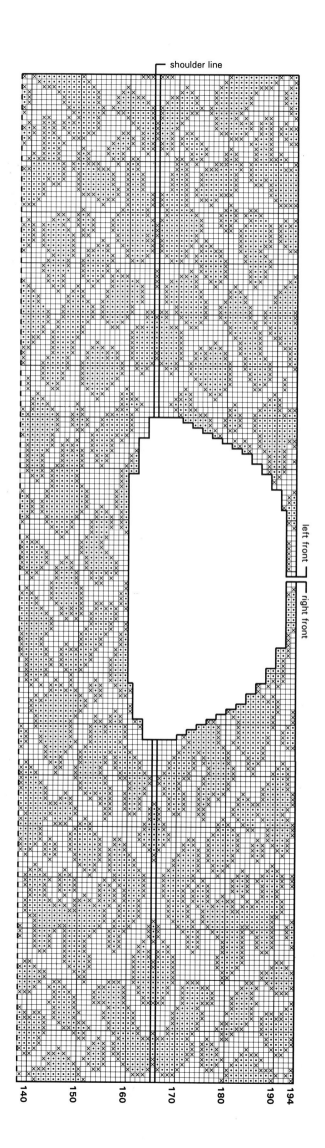

shoulder line

left front

right front

140 150 160 170 180 190 194

COLOUR SEQUENCE TABLE

Rows	☐	X	•	Rows	☐	X	•
1–2	B	V	U	91–93	T	Q	B
3–4	B	Q	U	94	T	E	B
5	B	Q	G	95–97	R	E	B
6	W	Q	G	98–99	R	E	C
7	W	Q	F	100	Y	E	C
8–10	H	Q	F	101	Y	E	F
11	U	Q	F	102	Y	V	F
12	U	Q	C	103–105	Y	V	N
13	T	Q	C	106–107	S	V	N
14	T	D	C	108–109	S	V	U
15	T	D	B	110–112	D	V	U
16	J	A	B	113–115	C	V	U
17–18	J	A	Y	116	C	V	H
19	T	A	Y	117	F	V	H
20–21	W	A	Y	118–119	F	V	L
22	H	A	Y	120–121	F	D	L
23–24	L	E	Y	122	F	D	T
25	H	E	C	123–125	U	D	T
26–27	U	E	C	126	W	V	T
28–29	N	E	C	127	B	V	T
30	N	E	W	128–129	B	V	U
31	F	E	W	130–131	B	Q	U
32–35	F	D	W	132	B	Q	G
36–37	C	D	W	133	W	Q	G
38–39	C	V	W	134	W	Q	F
40–41	R	V	W	135–137	H	Q	F
42–43	R	V	U	138	U	Q	F
44	R	V	H	139	U	Q	C
45–50	Y	V	H	140	T	Q	C
51	J	V	H	141	T	D	C
52	J	A	H	142	T	D	B
53–54	T	A	H	143	J	A	B
55–57	S	A	U	144–145	J	A	Y
58–59	W	A	U	146	T	A	Y
60–62	C	A	U	147–148	W	A	Y
63	F	A	U	149	H	A	Y
64–66	F	V	U	150–151	L	E	Y
67–68	F	V	T	152	H	E	C
69–71	F	V	S	153–154	U	E	C
72–76	U	V	S	155–156	N	E	C
77–78	H	V	S	157	N	E	W
79–80	L	D	S	158	F	E	W
81	H	D	W	159–162	F	D	W
82	T	D	W	163–164	C	D	W
83–87	J	A	W	165–166	C	V	W
88–90	J	Q	B				

Cast on at end of next row and foll alt rows, 2 sts twice, 3 sts once and 4 sts once **, ending with a WS row. (85 sts)

Cast on 13 sts at beg of next row. (98 sts)

Now work chart row 194, so ending with a WS row.

Cont foll chart from row 137 backwards down to row 1, matching colour sequence and patt as

before and marking side edge of row 96 for position of sleeve, so ending with a RS row. Change to 3mm (US 3) needles.
Next row (dec) (WS) Using 2 strands of yarn V, P2, (P2tog, P2tog, P1) 19 times, P1. (60 sts)
Work 21 rows in K1, P1 rib, reversing colour sequence given for back.
Cast (bind) off loosely and evenly in rib, using 2 strands of yarn A.
With WS facing, rejoin yarn to rem sts at neck edge, cast (bind) off 7 sts, work in patt to end.
Complete right front to match left front, reversing all shaping.

SLEEVES (both alike)

Cast on 49 sts, using 3mm (US 3) needles and 2 strands of yarn A.
Work 21 rows in K1, P1 rib in colour sequence as given for back, so ending with a RS row.
Next row (inc) (WS) Using 2 strands of yarn V, rib 3, M1, (rib 1, M1) 43 times, rib 3. (93 sts)
Change to 3¾mm (US 5) needles and (using one strand of each yarn) work 106 rows in patt from chart between markers for sleeve, and AT THE SAME TIME shape sides by inc one st at each end of 4th row and every foll 3rd row until there are 115 sts, then every foll 4th row until there are 145 sts, taking extra sts into patt as they occur.
Cast (bind) off loosely and evenly.

NECKBAND

Press all pieces gently on WS, using a warm iron over a damp cloth and avoiding ribbing.
With RS facing, using 3mm (US 3) needles and 2 strands of yarn V, pick up and K36 sts evenly up right front neck, 47 sts across back neck and 36 sts down left front neck. (119 sts)
Using 2 strands of each yarn, work 9 rows in K1, P1 rib in the foll colour sequence:
One row D, one row F, 2 rows U, one row T, 3 rows B and one row T.
Cast (bind) off loosely and evenly in rib, using 2 strands of yarn T.

BUTTON BAND

With RS facing, using 3mm (US 3) circular needle and 2 strands of yarn D, pick up and K130 sts evenly along left front edge for a woman's jacket or right front edge for a man's.
Using 2 strands of each yarn, work 7 rows in K1, P1 rib in the foll colour sequence:
One row F, 2 rows U, one row T and 3 rows B.
Cast (bind) off loosely and evenly in rib, using 2 strands of yarn C.

BUTTONHOLE BAND

Work as given for button band along other front, and AT THE SAME TIME work 8 buttonholes on rows 4 and 5 as foll:

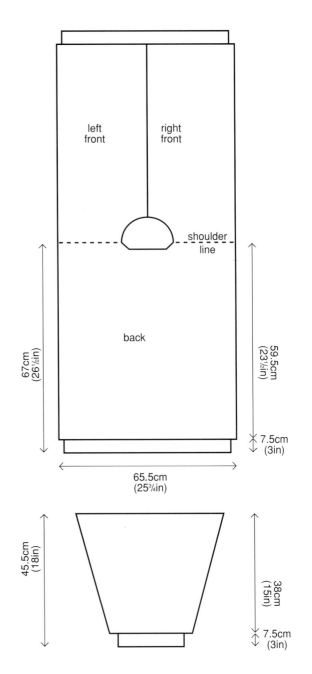

Row 4 (buttonholes) (RS) Using 2 strands of yarn T, rib 4, *cast (bind) off 3 sts, rib 14 including st already on needle after cast (bind) off,* rep from * to * 6 times more, cast (bind) off 3 sts, rib 4.
Row 5 Using 2 strands of yarn B, work in rib across row, casting on 3 sts to replace those cast (bound) off on previous row.

FINISHING

Using backstitch for all seams on main knitting and an edge to edge st for ribbing.
Set in sleeves between markers.
Join side and sleeve seams.
Sew on buttons to correspond with buttonholes.
Press seams.

HOUSES

Primitive houses in early American hooked rugs and patchwork quilts have always amused me. This sweater is the direct result of a visit to the American Museum in Bath, Avon, where I spotted a rag rug depicting many houses in a row – a perfect subject to adapt to the flat pattern of a knitted garment. The Donegal Tweeds suggest the feel of the colours used in the original hooked rug. This version is slightly brighter than my original, but I could see a far brighter rendition being even jollier. Think of the fresh colours in patchwork house patterns. This pattern also looks good on a chunkier scale – how about doubling the yarn or using an Aran weight yarn and larger needles to create a jacket, or even go to town on a houses bedcover!

SIZE AND MEASUREMENTS
One size to fit up to 97cm (38in) bust/chest
Finished measurement at underarm 111cm (43½in)
Length from shoulder 58cm (22¾in)

YARN
Rowan Botany – 25g (1oz) hanks, Lightweight DK – 25g (1oz) hanks, and Donegal Lambswool Tweed – 25g (1oz) hanks

The primitive house design of the Houses slipover is influenced by the American rag rug.

			Shade no	Amount
A	Botany		329	1 hank
B	Botany		77	1 hank
C	Botany		659	1 hank
D	Botany		118	1 hank
E	Botany		52	1 hank
F	Botany		70	1 hank
G	Botany		89	1 hank
H	Don Twd	Bay	485	1 hank
J	Don Twd	Bramble	484	3 hanks
L	Botany		632	1 hank
M	Don Twd	Rainforest	489	1 hank
N	Ltwt DK		55	1 hank
P	Don Twd	Tarragon	477	1 hank
Q	Don Twd	Sapphire	486	1 hank
R	Don Twd	Cinnamon	479	1 hank
S	Don Twd	Roseberry	480	1 hank
T	Don Twd	Dolphin	478	1 hank
U	Don Twd	Leaf	481	1 hank
V	Don Twd	Bark	475	1 hank
W	Don Twd	Pepper	473	1 hank
X	Don Twd	Nutmeg	470	1 hank
Y	Don Twd	Mist	466	1 hank
Z	Don Twd	Marram	472	1 hank

Note: Yarns are shown on the chart either by their relevant letters or by symbols. Refer to the chart key for symbols.

NEEDLES
Pair of 2¾mm (UK no 12) (US 2) needles
Pair of 3¼mm (UK no 10) (US 5) needles

TENSION/GAUGE
28 sts and 32 rows to 10cm (4in) measured over patterned st st using 3¼mm (US 3) needles. *Check your tension (gauge) carefully before beginning and change needle size if necessary.*

NOTES
Beginning at chart row 5, carry the yarn used for knitting the background, windows and doors (this colour is indicated at the side of the chart) right across the knitting (the fairisle method). It is advisable to link the main body of the house colour to the background colour at the upright vertical lines between the houses to obtain a strong join. When the background colour is not in use, carry it loosely across back

Note: Blank squares of background, windows and doors are worked in colour indicated at sides of chart

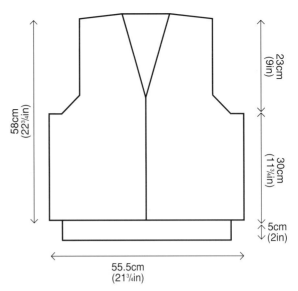

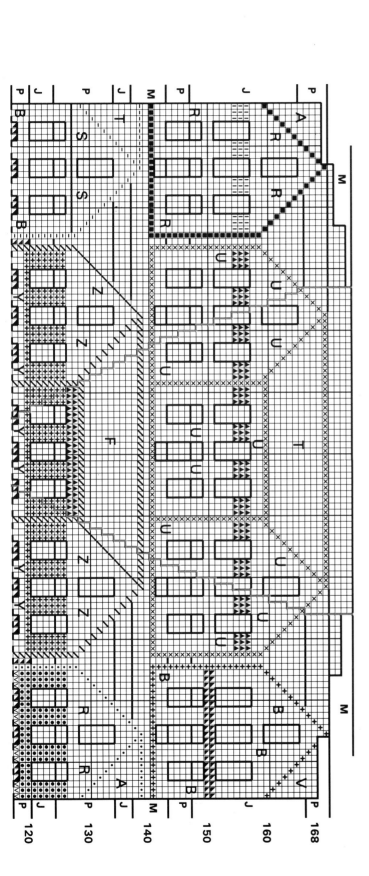

of the work, weaving in every 3 or 4 sts.
Use separate lengths of yarn (the intarsia method) for the outline colours and house colours.
Read chart from right to left for K (RS odd-numbered) rows and from left to right for P (WS even-numbered) rows.

BACK

Cast on 125 sts, using 2¾mm (US 2) needles and yarn A.
Work 17 rows in K1, P1 rib in the foll colour sequence:
2 rows J, one row L, one row B, 2 rows M, one row N, one row P, 2 rows Q, one row R, one row S, 2 rows M, one row J, one row T and one row U.
Next row (inc) (WS) Using yarn U, (rib 4, pick up horizontal loop before next st and work into back of it — called *make one* or *M1*) 30 times, rib 5. (155 sts)
Change to 3¼mm (US 3) needles and work in patt from chart (see Notes) for back which is worked entirely in st st, beg with a K row.
Work 94 rows in patt, so ending with a WS row.

Shape armholes

Foll chart throughout, cast (bind) off 14 sts at beg of next 2 rows and 2 sts at beg of next 4 rows.
Dec one st at beg of next 6 rows. (113 sts) **
Work without shaping until chart row 168 has been completed, so ending with a WS row.

Shape shoulders

Cast (bind) off 10 sts at beg of next 6 rows.
Leave rem 53 sts on a holder for back neck.

FRONT

Work as given for back to **.
Work 2 rows without shaping, so ending with a WS row.

Divide for front neck

Chart row 109 (RS) Work 54 sts in patt, K2tog, then turn and leave rem sts on a st holder.
Work each side of neck separately.

Work one row without shaping.
Dec one st at neck edge on next row and every foll alt row until there are 38 sts, then every foll 3rd row until there are 30 sts.
Work one row without shaping.

Shape shoulder
Cast (bind) off 10 sts at beg of next row and foll alt row.
Work one row without shaping.
Cast (bind) off rem 10 sts.
With RS facing, return to rem sts, leave centre st on safety pin, rejoin yarn to rem sts, K2tog, work in patt to end.
Complete to match first side of neck, reversing all shaping.

NECKBAND

Press both pieces gently on WS, using a warm iron over a damp cloth and avoiding ribbing.
Join right shoulder seam, using backstitch.
With RS facing, using 2¾mm (US 2) needles and yarn N, pick up and K64 sts down left front neck, K one st from safety pin (mark this with coloured thread), pick up and K64 sts up right front neck and K53 sts from st holder at centre back *but* dec to 52 sts by working 2 sts tog at centre. (181 sts)
Work in K1, P1 rib as foll:
Next row (WS) Using yarn M, * P1, K1, rep from * to within 2 sts of marked st, P2tog, P1 (centre st), P2tog tbl, (K1, P1) to end.
Next row Using yarn M, * K1, P1, rep from * to within 3 sts of marked st, K1, P2tog tbl, K1, P2tog, K1, (P1, K1) to end.
Rep last 2 rows 3 times more in the foll colour sequence:
One row M, one row B, one row L and 3 rows J.
Cast (bind) off evenly in rib, using yarn A and cont to dec one st either side of centre st as before.

ARMBANDS

Join left shoulder seam and neckband using backstitch for main knitting and an edge to edge st for ribbing.
With RS facing, using 2¾mm (US 2) needles and yarn J, pick up and K142 sts evenly around armhole edge.
P one row, using yarn S.
K 2 rows to form foldline, using yarn M.
Change to yarn J and work 4 rows in st st, beg with a K row.
Cast (bind) off loosely and evenly, using yarn J.

FINISHING

Join side seams and armbands, using backstitch.
Fold armhole facings to WS along foldline and slip stitch loosely in place.
Press seams.

Back view of the Houses slipover. This is knitted in a fine yarn, but the yarn could be doubled to produce a handsome jacket.

ZIGZAG

This is an old-time classic pattern that I never tire of – usually seen in bold, two-colour contrast, the zigzag is a perfect vehicle for shadings of two or three groups of colours. This relaxed cardigan has a striking yet subtle appearance that men enjoy wearing. It is knitted with only two colours in a row, making it among the easiest in this book.

SIZE AND MEASUREMENTS

One size to fit up to 107cm (42in) bust/chest
Finished measurement at underarm 127cm (50in)
Length from shoulder 72cm (28¼in)
Sleeve length 39.5cm (15½in)

YARN

Rowan Designer DK – 50g (1¾oz) balls, Donegal Lambswool Tweed – 25g (1oz) hanks, Lightweight DK – 25g (1oz) hanks, Lambswool Tweed – 50g (1¾oz) balls, and Kid Silk – 25g (1oz) balls

			Shade no	Amount
A	Des DK	Sage	669	1 ball
B	Des Dk	Petrol	672	1 ball
C	Des DK	Scarlet	673	1 ball
D	Des DK	Dusky Pink	70	1 ball
E	Ltwt DK		141	2 hanks
F	Des DK	Cherry	651	2 balls
G	Des DK	Violet	652	2 balls
H	Ltwt DK		91	2 hanks
J	Des DK	Forest	658	1 ball
K	Des DK	Chestnut	663	2 balls
L	Des DK	Burnt Orange	662	1 ball
M	Don Twd	Bramble	484	3 hanks
N	Don Twd	Bay	485	3 hanks
P	Lbs Twd	Dark Ore	183	1 ball
Q	Lbs Twd	Bluster	184	1 ball
R	Lbs Twd	Heliotrope	186	1 ball
S	Kid Silk	Smoke	998	1 ball
T	Kid Silk	Holly	990	1 ball
U	Kid Silk	Garnet	992	1 ball
V	Kid Silk	Old Gold	989	2 balls
W	Kid Silk	Crushed Berry	993	1 ball
X	Kid Silk	Pot-pourri	996	2 balls

Note: Yarns are shown on the chart either by their relevant letters or by symbols. Refer to the chart key for symbols.

NEEDLES AND BUTTONS

Pair of 3¾mm (UK no 9) (US 5) needles
Pair of 4mm (UK no 8) (US 6) needles
Circular needle 3¾mm (UK no 9) (US 5) 100cm (40in) long
Circular needle 4mm (UK no 8) (US 6) 100cm (40in) long
Seven buttons

TENSION/GAUGE

21 sts and 27 rows to 10cm (4in) measured over patterned st st using 4mm (US 6) needles.
Check your tension (gauge) carefully before beginning and change needle size if necessary.

NOTES

When working the colourwork pattern, use the fairisle method (2 colours a row), carrying yarn not in use loosely across back of work, weaving in every 3 or 4 sts and spreading sts to their correct width to keep them elastic.
Read chart from right to left for K (RS odd-numbered) rows and from left to right for P (WS even-numbered) rows unless otherwise stated.

BACK

Cast on 119 sts, using 3¾mm (US 5) needles and yarn M.
Work 21 rows in K1, P1 rib in the foll colour sequence:
One row F, 3 rows B, one row R, 2 rows K, one row D, 3 rows G, 2 rows M, one row Q, 2 rows X, one row A, one row W, 2 rows H and one row F.
Next row (inc) (WS) Using yarn F, rib 7, (pick up horizontal loop before next st and work into back of it — called *make one or M1 —*, rib 8) 14 times. (133 sts)
Change to 4mm (US 6) needles and cont in patt from chart (see Notes) for back which is worked entirely in st st, beg with a K row.
Work 88 rows in patt, marking each end of rows 10 and 52 for pocket openings, so ending with a WS row.
Shape armholes
Next row (RS) K2tog, work in patt to last 2 sts, K2tog tbl.
Next row Work in patt to end.
Foll chart throughout for patt, rep these 2 rows until chart row 176 has been completed.
Leave rem 45 sts on a st holder.

LEFT FRONT

Cast on 59 sts, using 3¾mm (US 5) needles and yarn M.
Work 21 rows in K1, P1 rib as given for back.
Next row (inc) (WS) Using yarn F, rib 3, (M1, rib 7) 8 times. (67 sts)
Change to 4mm (US 6) needles and work 88 rows in patt from chart between markers for left front, marking positions of pocket opening on side edge as for back, so ending with a WS row.

The Zigzag jacket is a relaxed design, with a striking pattern in two colours, that I enjoy wearing.

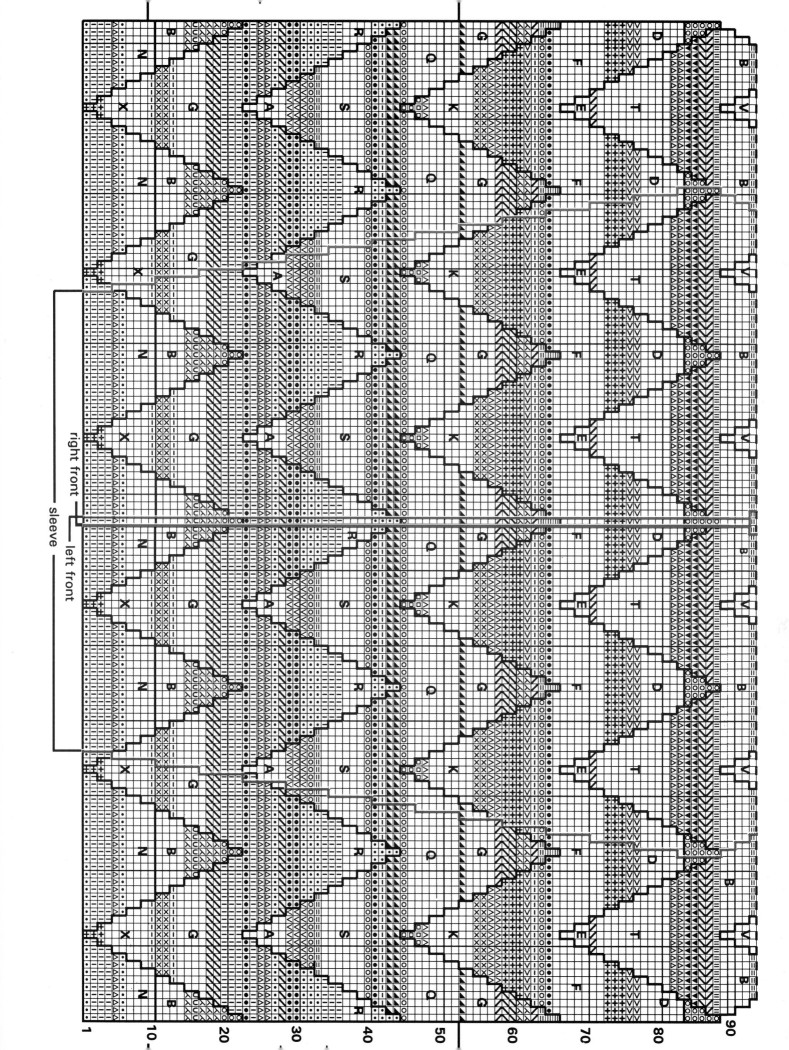

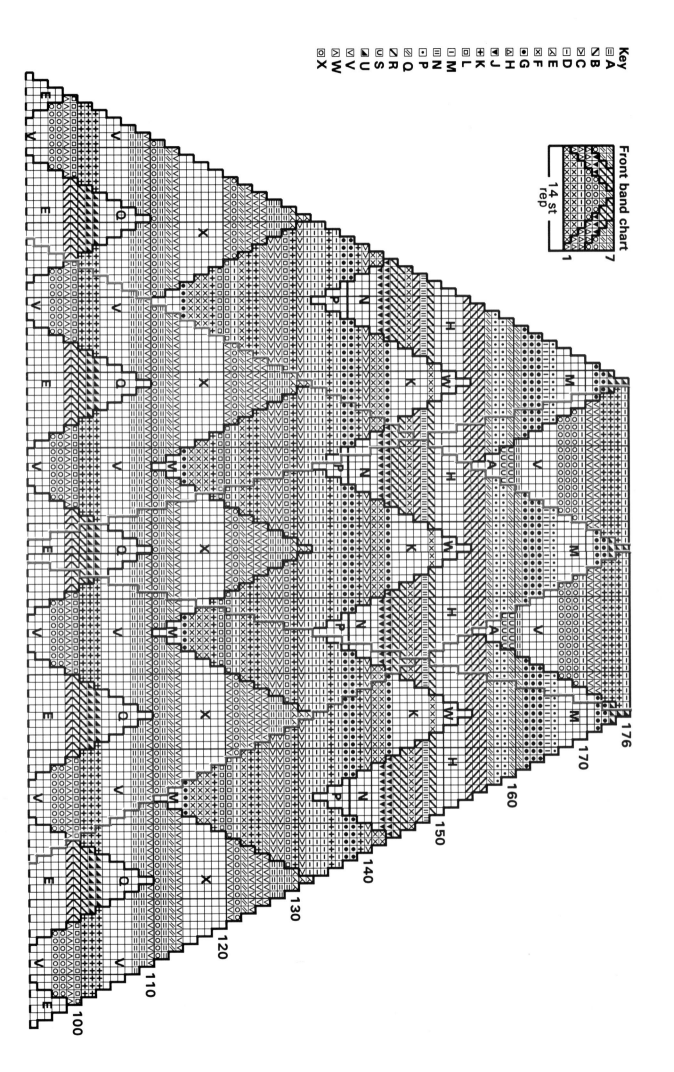

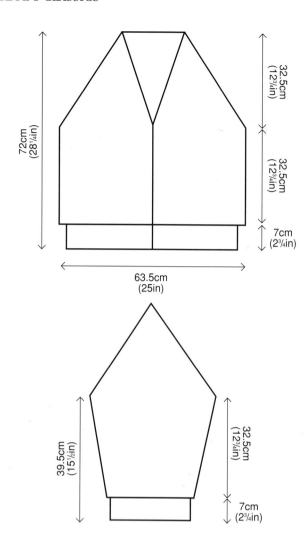

Shape armhole and front neck

Next row (RS) K2tog, work in patt to last 2 sts, K2tog tbl.
Next row Work in patt to end.
Next row K2tog, work in patt to end.
Next row Work in patt to end.
Foll chart throughout, rep these 4 rows until 176 rows have been completed and one st rem.
Leave st on a st holder.

RIGHT FRONT

Work as given for left front, reversing all shaping and foll chart between markers for right front.

SLEEVES (both alike)

Cast on 53 sts, using 3¾mm (US 5) needles and yarn M.
Work 21 rows in K1, P1 rib as given for back.
Next row (inc) (WS) Rib 5, (M1, rib 6) 8 times. (61 sts)
Change to 4mm (US 6) needles and work 88 rows in patt from chart between markers for sleeve, and AT THE SAME TIME shape sides by inc one st at each end of 5th row and every foll 6th row until there are 89 sts, taking extra sts into patt as they occur.

Shape sleeve top

Next row (RS) K2tog, work in patt to last 2 sts, K2tog tbl.

Next row Work in patt to end.
Foll chart throughout, rep these 2 rows until chart row 174 has been completed and 3 sts rem.
Next row (RS) K3tog.
Leave rem st on a st holder.

POCKET EDGINGS (both alike)

Press all pieces gently on WS, using a warm iron over a damp cloth and avoiding ribbing.
With RS facing, using 3¾mm (US 5) needles and yarn M, pick up and K36 sts evenly between markers on side edge of front.
K 2 rows to form foldline.
Change to yarn F and work 5 rows in st st, beg with a P row.
Cast (bind) off evenly.

POCKET LININGS

With RS facing, using 4mm (US 6) needles and yarn F, pick up and K36 sts evenly between markers on left side edge of back and work in st st, beg with a P row, and AT THE SAME TIME cast on 6 sts at beg of first row and dec one st at beg of 2nd row and every foll alt row until 24 sts rem.
Cast (bind) off evenly.
Work right pocket lining as given for left pocket lining, reversing all shaping.

FRONT BANDS (worked in one piece)

Join raglan shoulder seams, using backstitch.
With RS facing, using 4mm (US 6) circular needle and yarn F, beg at lower right front edge and pick up and K18 sts evenly to top of rib, 80 sts up right front edge to beg of neck shaping, 80 sts up right neck edge, K1 st from st holder at top of right front, K1 st from st holder at top of sleeve, K45 sts from st holder at back neck inc one st at centre to make 46 sts, K1 st from st holder at top of left sleeve, K1 st from st holder at top of left front, pick up and K80 sts down left neck edge to beg of neck shaping, 80 sts down left front edge to top of rib and 18 sts down rib. (406 sts)
Working back and forth in rows (not rounds), work 7 rows in patt from chart for front band, beg row 1 at left hand side of chart with a P row and rep 14 st patt 29 times across row, and AT THE SAME TIME make 7 buttonholes on chart rows 2 and 3 as foll:

Man's version only:
Next row (buttonholes) (RS) Work 310 sts in patt, cast (bind) off 2 sts, *work 13 sts in patt including st already on needle after cast (bind) off, cast (bind) off 2 sts,* rep from * to * 5 times more, work in patt to end.

Woman's version only:
Next row (buttonholes) (RS) Work 4 sts in patt, cast (bind) off 2 sts, * work 13 sts in patt including st already on needle after cast (bind) off, cast (bind) off 2 sts,* rep from * to * 5 times more, work in patt to end.

Both versions:

Next row (WS) Work in patt, casting on 2 sts to replace those cast (bound) off on previous row. After 7 chart rows have been completed, change to 3¾mm (US 5) circular needle and yarn M and K 3 rows to form foldline.

Change to yarn F and beg with a P row, work 9 rows in st st, and AT THE SAME TIME work 7 buttonholes on rows 4 and 5 to correspond with those already made. Cast (bind) off evenly.

FINISHING

Use backstitch for all seams on main knitting and an edge to edge st for ribbing.

Women as well as men look good in the Zigzag jacket, worn here with strong colours that tone perfectly.

Join sleeve seams and side seams above and below pockets.

Fold pocket edgings to WS along foldline and slip stitch loosely in place.

Slip stitch pocket linings loosely to WS of fronts.

Fold front bands and neckband in half to WS along foldline and slip stitch in place.

Sew buttons to button band to correspond with buttonholes.

Press seams.

FOOLISH VIRGINS

When my retrospective show (first staged by the Victoria & Albert Museum in London) travelled to Norway I had a chance to look in depth at the decorative arts in their splendid museum in Oslo. Many versions of these Foolish Virgins tapestries were woven when everyone knew their Bible better! This is a cotton version but I have also done a Kid Silk and wool darker colourway. It would be fun to make this a riot of contrasting colours. Each area of the design is a simple two-colour-a-row exercise.

SIZE AND MEASUREMENTS
One size to fit up to 102cm (40in) bust/chest
Finished measurement at underarm 112cm (52in)
Jacket length from shoulder 50cm (19¾in)
Jacket sleeve length 44.5cm (17½in)
Crewneck length from shoulder 69.5cm (27½in)
Crewneck sleeve length 50.5cm (19¾in)

YARN
Rowan Cotton Glacé – 50g (1¾oz) balls
(Jacket amounts are in brackets)

			Shade no	Amount
A	Glacé	Black	727	4[4] balls
B	Glacé	Gentian	743	2[2] balls
C	Glacé	Quince	745	1[1] ball
D	Glacé	Clay	738	2[3] balls
E	Glacé	Rowan	736	1[1] ball
F	Glacé	Provence	744	2[2] balls
G	Glacé	Harebell	732	2[2] balls
H	Glacé	Water Melon	740	2[2] balls
J	Glacé	Spice	737	1[1] ball
M	Glacé	Putty	733	1[1] ball
N	Glacé	Dijon	739	2[2] balls
O	Glacé	Matador	742	2[2] balls
V	Glacé	Navy	729	1[1] ball
X	Glacé	Poppy	741	3[3] balls

Note: Yarns are shown on the charts either by their relevant letters or by symbols. Refer to the chart key for symbols.

NEEDLES AND FASTENERS
Pair of 3¼mm (UK no 10) (US 3) needles
Pair of 3¾mm (UK no 9) (US 5) needles
3.00mm (US size D) crochet hook for jacket
Eight clasp fasteners for jacket

TENSION/GAUGE
23 sts and 28 rows to 10cm (4in) measured over patterned st st using 3¾mm (US 5) needles.
Check your tension (gauge) carefully before beginning and change needle size if necessary.

NOTES
When working the colourwork pattern, use the intarsia method, using a separate length of yarn for each area of contrasting colour and linking one colour to the next by twisting them around each other where they meet on WS to avoid holes.
Read chart from right to left for K (RS odd-numbered) rows and from left to right for P (WS even-numbered) rows.

THE JACKET
BACK
Cast on 140 sts, using 3¼mm (US 3) needles and yarn B.
Work 8 rows in st st, beg with a K row.
Purl one row (RS) to form hemline fold.
Next row (inc) (WS) P3, (P into front and back of next st — called *inc 1* —, P11) 11 times, inc 1 in next st, P4. (152 sts)
Change to 3¾mm (US 5) needles and cont in patt from chart (see Notes) for back which is worked entirely in st st, beg with a K row.
Work 140 rows in patt, marking each end of rows 7 and 43 for pocket openings, so ending with a WS row.
Shape shoulders
Foll chart throughout, cast (bind) off 18 sts at beg of next 6 rows.
Cast (bind) off rem 44 sts.

LEFT FRONT
Cast on 70 sts, using 3¼mm (US 3) needles and yarn B.
Work 8 rows in st st, beg with a K row.
Purl one row (RS) to form hemline fold.
Next row (inc) (WS) P5, (inc 1 in next st, P11) 5 times, inc 1 in next st, P4. (76 sts)
Change to 3¾mm (US 5) needles and work 121 rows in patt from chart between markers for left front, marking position of pocket opening on side edge as for back, so ending with a RS row.
Shape front neck
Foll chart throughout, cast (bind) off 5 sts at beg of next row. Work one row without shaping.
Dec one st at neck edge on next 17 rows. (54 sts)
Shape shoulder
Cast (bind) off 18 sts at beg of next row and foll alt row.
Work one row without shaping.
Cast (bind) off rem 18 sts.

RIGHT FRONT
Work as given for left front, reversing all shaping and foll chart between markers for right front.

The Foolish Virgins crewneck and jacket pictured here make me think of a Slavic peasant wedding scene.

SLEEVES (both alike)

Cast on 47 sts, using 3¼mm (US 3) needles and yarn B.

Work 8 rows in st st, beg with a K row.

Purl one row (RS) to form hemline fold.

Next row (inc) (WS) P3, (inc 1 in next st, P7) 5 times, inc 1 in next st, P3. (53 sts)

**Change to 3¾mm (US 5) needles and work 121 rows in patt from chart for sleeve, and AT THE SAME TIME shape sides by inc one st at each end of 5th row and every foll 3rd row until there are 131 sts, taking extra sts into patt as they occur. (Please note that the top right-hand edge of sleeve is shown as a sleeve extension at the side of the chart.)

Row 122 Purl, working 4J, (3A, 3J) 21 times, 1J.

Row 123 Knit, working 2J, (1A, 1J) 64 times, 1J.

Row 124 As row 122.

Cast (bind) off loosely and evenly, using yarn A.

POCKET EDGINGS (both alike)

Press all pieces gently on WS, using a warm iron over a damp cloth and avoiding ribbing.

With RS facing, using 3¼mm (US 3) needles and yarn A, pick up and K34 sts evenly between markers on side edge of front.

K one row (WS) to form foldline.

Work 4 rows in st st, beg with a K row.

Cast (bind) off loosely and evenly.

POCKET LININGS

With RS facing, using 3¾mm (US 5) needles and yarn A, pick up and K34 sts evenly between markers on left side edge of back and work in st st, beg with a P row, and AT THE SAME TIME cast on 5 sts at beg of first row and dec one st at beg of 2nd row and every foll alt row until 24 sts rem.

Cast (bind) off evenly.

Work right pocket lining as given for left pocket lining, reversing all shaping.

FRONT BANDS (both alike)

With RS facing, using 3¾mm (US 5) needles and yarn B, pick up and K92 sts evenly along front edge.

K one row (WS) to form foldline.

Change to 3¼mm (US 3) needles and work 8 rows in st st, beg with a K row.

Cast (bind) off evenly.

COLLAR

Cast on 100 sts, using 3¼mm (US 3) needles and yarn A.

Then, using the intarsia method, work in patt as foll:

Row 1 (RS) K20, using yarn C, K20 using yarn X, K20 using yarn N, K20 using yarn H, K20 using yarn F.

Row 2 P20 F, P20 H, P20 N, P20 X, P20 C.

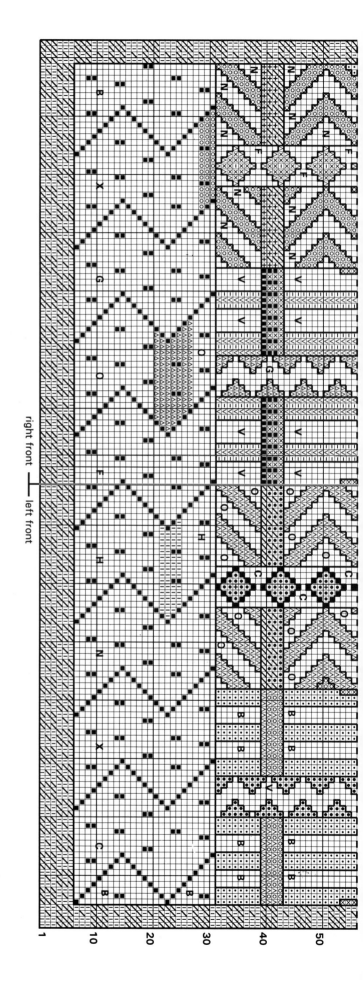

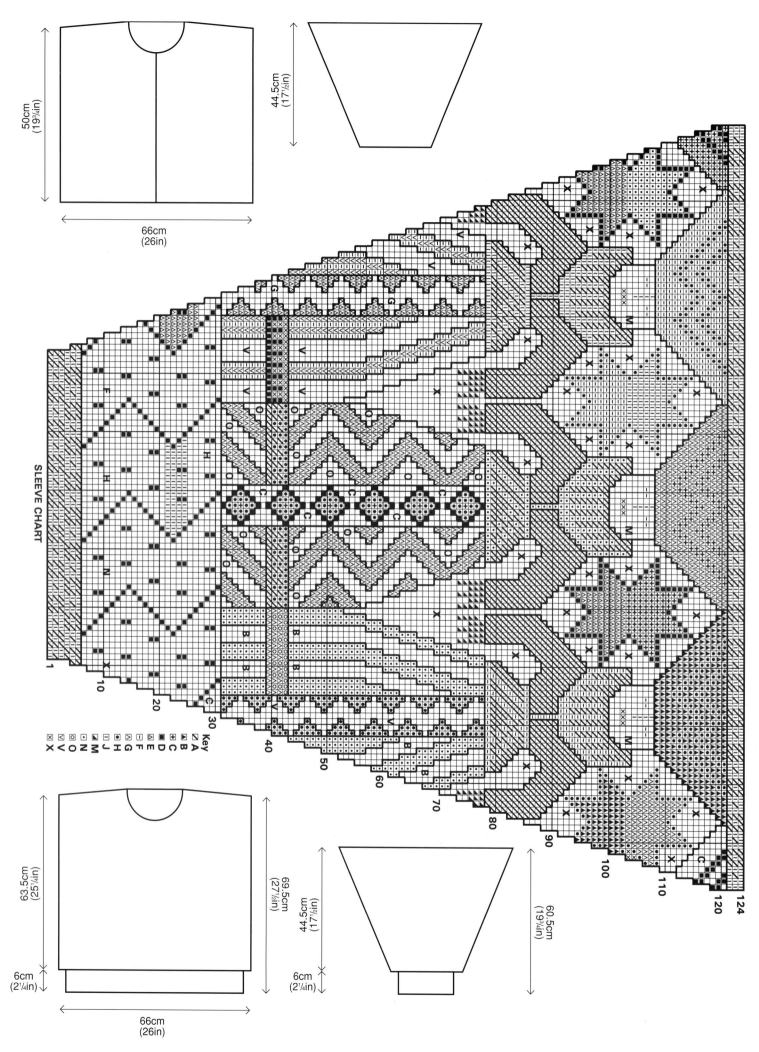

50cm
(19¾in)

66cm
(26in)

44.5cm
(17½in)

SLEEVE CHART

63.5cm
(25in)

69.5cm
(27½in)

6cm
(2¼in)

66cm
(26in)

44.5cm
(17½in)

60.5cm
(19¾in)

6cm
(2¼in)

Key
⊠ A
◪ B
⊡ C
⊞ D
◼ E
⊡ F
◪ G
◨ H
⊡ J
◪ M
◒ N
○ O
◩ V
✕ X

1 10 20 30 40 50 60 70 80 90 100 110 120 124

Keeping to stripe patt as set in last 2 rows throughout, work 4 rows more in st st, so ending with a WS row.

Shape collar

Cast (bind) off 4 sts at beg of next 14 rows.

Cast (bind) off rem 44 sts evenly in patt.

FINISHING

Use backstitch for all seams on main knitting and an edge to edge st for ribbing.

Join both shoulder seams.

Fold front bands to WS along foldline and slip stitch loosely in place.

Sew shaped edge of collar to neckline.

Collar edging

With RS facing and crochet hook, join yarn B to collar edge, work 4ch, ** 1 dc (US sc) into each of next 2 sts, 4ch; rep from ** to end, finishing with 2dc (US sc), turn and work 5dc (US sc) into each 4ch space to end. Fasten off.

Place markers 28cm (11¼in) down from shoulder seam on back and fronts.

Set in sleeve between markers.

Join sleeve seams and side seams above and below pocket.

Fold pocket edgings to WS along foldline and slip stitch loosely in place.

Slip stitch pocket linings loosely to WS of fronts.

Sew on clasp fasteners.

Press seams.

THE CREWNECK

BACK

Cast on 122 sts, using 3¼mm (US 3) needles and yarn B.

Work 20 rows in K1, P1 rib in the foll colour sequence:

2 rows O, one row X, one row N, one row V, 2 rows C, 2 rows F, 2 rows B, 2 rows F, 2 rows C, one row V, one row N, one row X and 2 rows O.

Next row (inc) (WS) Using yarn B, rib 3, (pick up horizontal loop before next st and work into back of it — called *make one* or *M1* —, rib 4) 29 times, M1, rib 3. (152 sts)

Change to 3¾mm (US 5) needles and cont in patt from chart (see Notes) for back which is worked entirely in st st, beg with a K row.**

Work 178 rows in patt, so ending with a WS row.

Shape shoulders

Foll chart throughout, cast (bind) off 18 sts at beg of next 6 rows.

Cast (bind) off rem 44 sts.

FRONT

Work as given for back to **.

Work 156 rows in patt from chart for front, so ending with a WS row.

Shape front neck

Chart row 157 (RS) Work 69 sts in patt, then turn and leave rem sts on a st holder.

Work each side of neck separately, foll chart throughout.

Dec one st at neck edge on next 12 rows, then on foll 3 alt rows. (54 sts)

Shape shoulder

Cast (bind) off 18 sts at beg of next row and foll alt row.

Work one row without shaping.

Cast (bind) off rem 18 sts.

With RS facing, rejoin yarn to rem sts, cast (bind) off centre 14 sts, work in patt to end.

Complete to match first side of neck, reversing all shaping.

SLEEVES (both alike)

Cast on 53 sts, using 3¼mm (US 3) needles and yarn B.

Work 20 rows in K1, P1 rib in colour sequence as given for back, then rib one row using yarn B.

Complete as for sleeves for jacket from ** (see page 118).

NECKBAND

Press all pieces gently on WS, using a warm iron over a damp cloth and avoiding ribbing.

Join right shoulder seam, using backstitch.

With RS facing, using 3¼mm (US 3) needles and yarn B, pick up and K26 sts evenly down left front neck, 14 sts across centre front, 26 sts up right front neck and 44 sts across back neck. (110 sts)

Work 8 rows in K1, P1 rib in the foll colour sequence:

One row F, one row C, one row V, one row N, one row X, 2 rows O and one row B.

Cast (bind) off evenly in rib, using yarn B.

FINISHING

Use backstitch for all seams on main knitting and an edge to edge st for ribbing.

Join left shoulder seam and neckband.

Place markers 28cm (11¼in) down from shoulder seam on back and front.

Set in sleeves between markers.

Join side and sleeve seams.

Press seams.

SPANISH COMBS

Despite the name, the inspiration for this comes from a book on Japanese brocades which I often look at for ideas. Although it appears dainty and intricate to knit, many beginners have attempted it with great success. When I had finished it, it somehow suggested the high Spanish combs I remember seeing on Flamenco dancers as a child.

SIZE AND MEASUREMENTS

One size to fit up to 122cm (48in) bust
Finished measurement at underarm 140cm (55in)
Length from shoulder 69cm (27¼in)
Sleeve length 43cm (17in)

YARN

Rowan Kid Silk, Rowan Donegal Lambswool Tweed, and Rowan Lightweight DK – all 25g (1oz) balls/hanks

			Shade no	Amount
A	Kid Silk	Turnip	997	6 balls
B	Kid Silk	Potpourri	996	1 ball
C	Don Twd	Nutmeg	470	6 hanks
D	Don Twd	Mist	466	1 hank
E	Don Twd	Roseberry	480	1 hank
F	Ltwt DK		104	2 hanks
G	Ltwt DK		620	1 hank
H	Ltwt DK		72	1 hank
J	Ltwt DK		8	2 hanks
L	Ltwt DK		5	1 hank
N	Ltwt DK		100	1 hank
Q	Ltwt DK		417	2 hanks
R	Ltwt DK		75	1 hank
S	Ltwt DK		32	1 hank
T	Ltwt DK		76	1 hank
U	Ltwt DK		49	1 hank
W	Ltwt DK		63	1 hank
Y	Ltwt DK		47	2 hanks
Z	Ltwt DK		78	1 hank
a	Ltwt DK		403	2 hanks
b	Ltwt DK		79	2 hanks
d	Ltwt DK		615	2 hanks
e	Ltwt DK		83	3 hanks
f	Ltwt DK		121	1 hank
g	Ltwt DK		69	1 hank
n	Ltwt DK		92	1 hank
r	Ltwt DK		109	2 hanks

Note: Yarns are shown on the charts either by their relevant letters or by symbols. Refer to the chart key for symbols.

NEEDLES

Pair of 3¼mm (UK no 10) (US 3) needles
Pair of 4mm (UK no 8) (US 6) needles

TENSION/GAUGE

27 sts and 27 rows to 10cm (4in) measured over patterned st st using 4mm (US 6) needles.
Check your tension (gauge) carefully before beginning and change needle size if necessary.

NOTES

The pattern is comprised of a series of interlocking comb motifs, each being shaded by horizontal bands of colour which go right across their width.
Use separate lengths of yarn (the intarsia method) for each band of colour within the motifs, linking one colour to the next by twisting them around each other where they meet on WS to avoid holes.
Carry the yarns A, C and F, which are used for the outlines and central blocks to the comb motifs, loosely right across the back of the work, weaving them in every 3 or 4 sts (the fairisle method).
Read charts from right to left for K (RS odd-numbered) rows and from left to right for P (WS even-numbered) rows.

BACK

Cast on 151 sts, using 3¼mm (US 3) needles and yarn B.
Work 35 rows in K1, P1 rib in the foll colour sequence:
One row d, 2 rows N, one row Q, one row d, 3 rows A, one row f, 2 rows W, one row L, one row G, 3 rows J, one row n, one row d, 2 rows Q, one row W, one row H, 3 rows F, one row e, one row f, 3 rows g, one row r, 2 rows A and 2 rows U.
Next row (inc) (WS) Using yarn C, P2, pick up loop before next st and purl into back of it — called *make one purlwise or M1P —*, (P4, M1p) 37 times, P1. (189 sts)
Change to 4mm (US 6) needles and cont in patt from chart (see Notes) for back which is worked entirely in st st, beg with a K row. **
Work 162 rows in patt, marking each end of row 78 for position of sleeve, so ending with a WS row.

Shape shoulders and neck

Foll chart throughout, cast (bind) off 18 sts at beg of next 2 rows.
Chart row 165 (RS) Cast (bind) off 17 sts, work 45 sts in patt including st already on needle after cast (bind) off, then turn and leave rem sts on a st holder.
Work each side of neck separately.
Cast (bind) off 5 sts at beg of next row, 17 sts at beg of foll row, and 5 sts at beg of next row.

The Spanish Combs crewneck is set off to perfection here by the aging textures of this abandoned Baptist Chapel.

Key □A ☒B ⊡C ⊞D ▥E ⊡F ⊠G ⊟H ⊠J ⊠L ⊠N ⊡Q ⊠R ⊠S ▨T ⊠U ▨W ▤Y ⊡a ⊡b ☒d ⊡e ⊠f ⊡g ⊟n ⊠r
Note : Blank squares are worked in colour marked on chart by relevent letter.

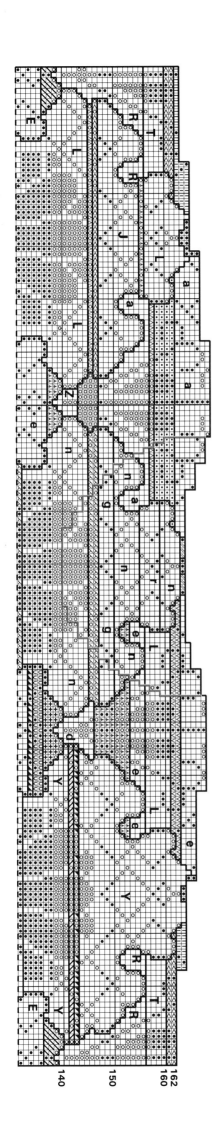

Cast (bind) off rem 18 sts.
With RS facing, rejoin yarn to rem sts, cast (bind) off centre 29 sts for centre back neck, work in patt to end.
Complete to match first side of neck, reversing all shaping.

FRONT

Work as given for back to **.
Work 140 rows in patt from chart for front, marking each end of row 78 for position of sleeve, so ending with a WS row.
Shape front neck
Chart row 141 (RS) Work 87 sts in patt, then turn and leave rem sts on a st holder.
Work each side of neck separately, foll chart throughout.
Cast (bind) off at beg of next row and foll alt rows, 3 sts twice, 2 sts 3 times and one st 5 times. (70 sts)
Cont without shaping until front matches back to shoulder, ending with a WS row.
Shape shoulder
Cast (bind) off 18 sts at beg of next row and 17 sts at beg of foll 2 alt rows.
Work one row without shaping.
Cast (bind) off rem 18 sts.
With RS facing, rejoin yarn to rem sts, cast (bind) off centre 15 sts, work in patt to end.
Work one row without shaping.
Complete to match first side of neck, reversing all shaping.

SLEEVES (both alike)

Cast on 57 sts, using 3¼mm (US 3) needles and yarn B.
Work 35 rows in K1, P1 rib in colour sequence as given for back.
Next row (inc) (WS) Using yarn C, [P2, M1p, (P1, M1p) 3 times] 11 times, P2. (101 sts)
Change to 4mm (US 6) needles and work 92 rows in patt from chart for sleeve, and AT THE SAME TIME shape sides by inc one st at each end of 3rd row and every foll alt row until there are 145 sts, then at each end of every foll 3rd row until there are 169 sts, taking all increased sts into patt as they occur.
Cast (bind) off loosely and evenly.

NECKBAND

Press all pieces gently on WS, using a warm iron over a damp cloth and avoiding ribbing.
Join right shoulder seam, using backstitch.
With RS facing, 3¼mm (US 3) needles and yarn U, pick up and K33 sts evenly down left front neck, 15 sts across centre front, 33 sts up right front neck and 50 sts across back neck. (131 sts)
Work 7 rows in K1, P1 rib in the foll colour sequence:

KAFFE'S CLASSICS

One row U, 2 rows H, 2 rows B, one row d and
one row N.
Cast (bind) off evenly in rib, using yarn Q.

FINISHING

Use backstitch for all seams on main knitting and
an edge to edge st for ribbing.
Join left shoulder seam and neckband.
Set in sleeves between markers.
Join side and sleeve seams.
Press seams.

Note : Blank squares are worked in colour marked on chart by relevent letter.

SLEEVE CHART

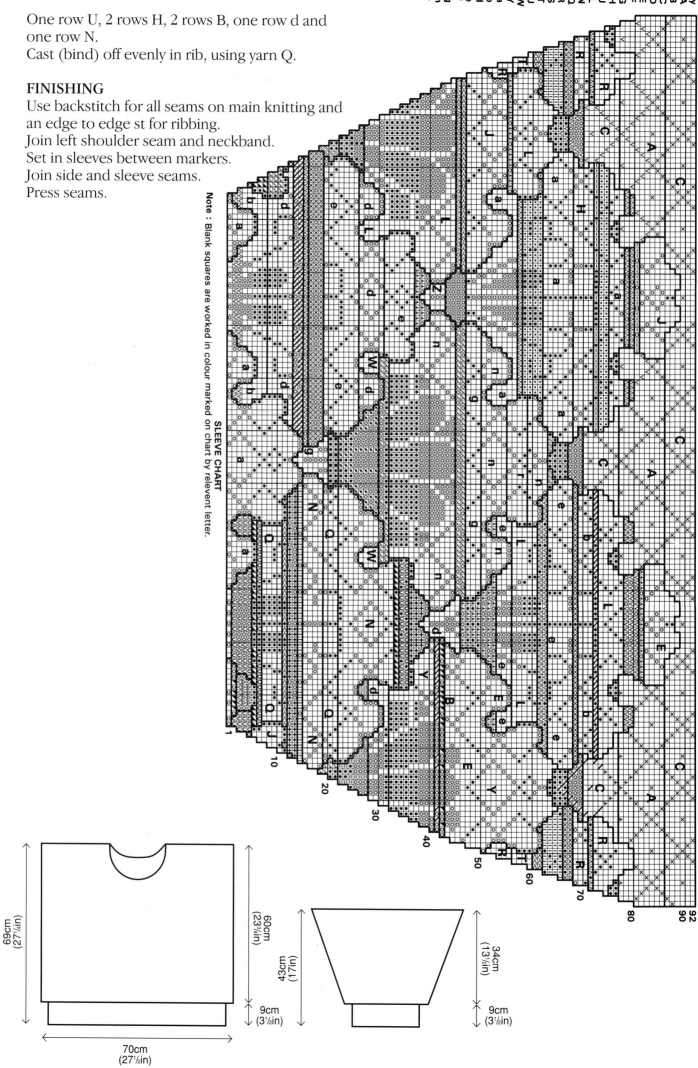

ICON

The world of Russian icons is a powerful source of inspiration for colours and patterns. The black and white crosses on the priests' robes have often attracted me for their bold contrast. When I began to do my version in wool, the jewel colours excited me and the use of contrast outline delineates the colours wonderfully. Please do have a go at your own colours – perhaps dusty pastels on dark tweeds?

SIZE AND MEASUREMENTS

One size to fit up to 102cm (40in) bust/chest
Finished measurement at underarm 117cm (46in)
Length from shoulder 65cm (25½in)
Sleeve length 50.5cm (21in)

YARN

Rowan Lightweight DK – 25g (1oz) hanks

		Shade no	Amount
A	Ltwt DK	50	1 hank
B	Ltwt DK	57	2 hanks
C	Ltwt DK	52	3 hanks
D	Ltwt DK	93	2 hanks
E	Ltwt DK	94	1 hank
F	Ltwt DK	96	1 hank
G	Ltwt DK	27	2 hanks
H	Ltwt DK	46	2 hanks
J	Ltwt DK	602	3 hanks
K	Ltwt DK	73	2 hanks
L	Ltwt DK	99	2 hanks
M	Ltwt DK	405	1 hank
N	Ltwt DK	9	2 hanks
O	Ltwt DK	407	2 hanks
P	Ltwt DK	62	4 hanks
R	Ltwt DK	404	1 hank
S	Ltwt DK	97	1 hank
T	Ltwt DK	100	2 hanks
W	Ltwt DK	54	2 hanks

Note: Yarns are shown on the chart either by their relevant letters or by symbols. Refer to the chart key for symbols.

NEEDLES

Pair of 3mm (UK no 11) (US 3) needles
Pair of 3¾mm (UK no 9) (US 5) needles

TENSION/GAUGE

24 sts and 31 rows to 10cm (4in) measured over patterned st st using 3¾mm (US 5) knitting needles.
Check your tension (gauge) carefully before beginning your knitting and change needle size if necessary.

The Icon crewneck, a delight to knit with its contrasting, vivid outlines.

NOTES

When working the colourwork pattern, use the intarsia method, using a separate length of yarn for each area of contrasting colour and linking one colour to the next by twisting them around each other where they meet on WS to avoid holes.
Read chart from right to left for K (RS odd-numbered) rows and from left to right for P (WS even-numbered) rows unless otherwise stated.

BACK

Cast on 138 sts, using 3mm (US 3) needles and yarn J.
Change to yarns C and P and work in 2 colour rib as foll:
Row 1 (RS) (K2C, P2P) to last 2 sts, K2C.
Row 2 (P2C, K2P) to last 2 sts, P2C.
Rep these 2 rows until work measures 7.5cm (3in) from beg, ending with a RS row.
Next row (inc) (WS) Using yarn P only, P1, pick up horizontal loop before next st and purl into back of it — called *make one purlwise or M1p* —, P136, M1p, P1. (140 sts)
Change to 3¾mm (US 5) needles and cont in patt from chart (see Notes) for back which is worked

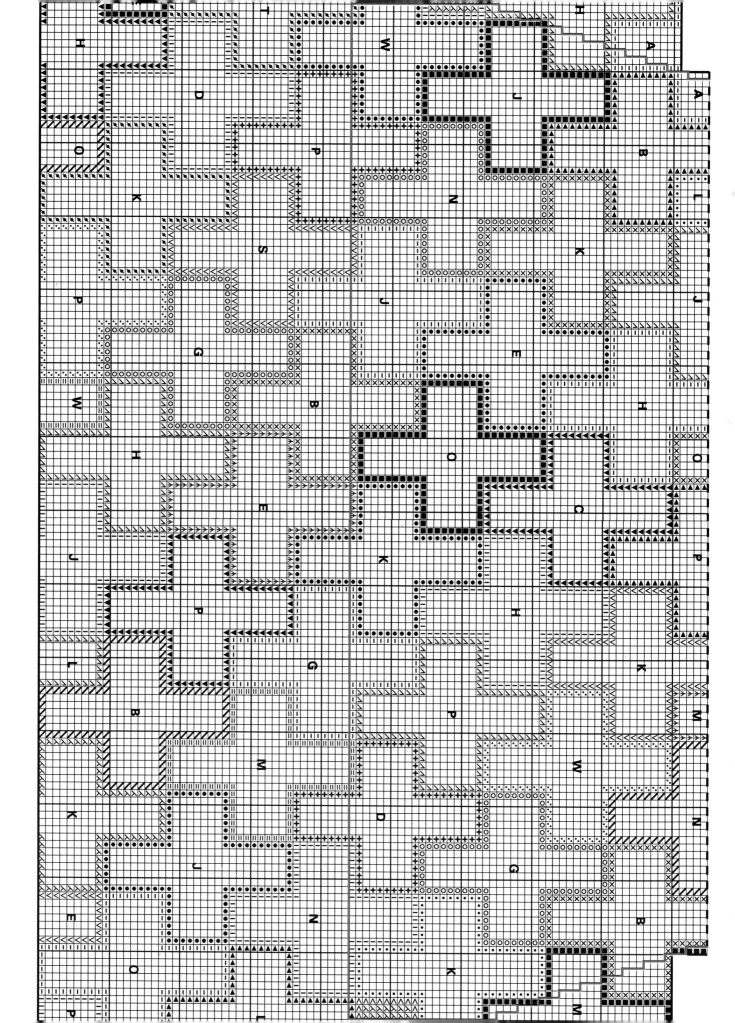

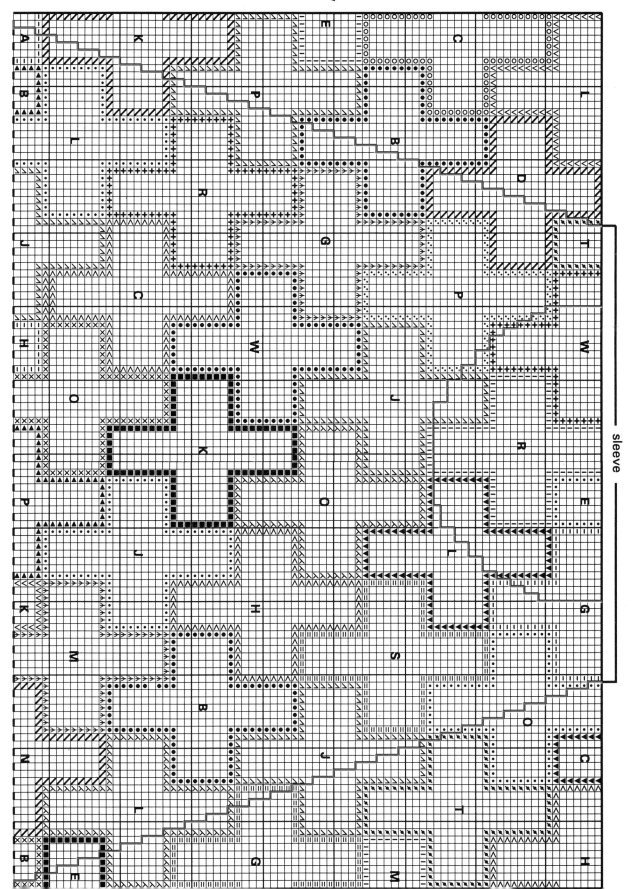

sleeve

Key
A ·
B —
C ·
D ⊠
E ◹
F ◺
G +
H ◿
J ◣
K ‖
L ◢
M ▼
N ◿
O O
P ■
R ▷
S ·
T ·
W ·

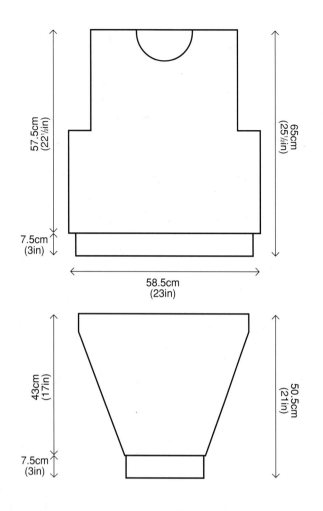

entirely in st st, beg with a K row.
Work 90 rows in patt, so ending with a WS row.
Shape armholes
Foll chart throughout, cast (bind) off 10 sts at beg of next 2 rows. (120 sts) **
Cont without shaping until chart row 178 has been completed.
Cast (bind) off evenly.

FRONT
Work as given for back to **.
Cont without shaping until chart row 154 has been completed, so ending with a WS row.
Shape front neck
Chart row 155 (RS) Work 53 sts in patt, then turn and leave rem sts on a st holder.
Work each side of neck separately.
Cast (bind) off 3 sts at beg of next row and 2 sts at beg of foll 3 alt rows.
Work one row without shaping.
Dec one st at neck edge on next row and foll 3 alt rows. (40 sts)

Cont without shaping until front matches back to shoulder, ending with a WS row.
Cast (bind) off evenly.
With RS facing, rejoin yarn to rem sts, cast (bind) off centre 14 sts, work in patt patt to end.
Work one row without shaping.
Complete to match first side of neck, reversing all shaping.

SLEEVES (both alike)
The sleeve is inverted on the chart, but it is knitted conventionally from cuff to top, therefore it is best to turn the chart upside down to work the sleeve – but take care to read the symbols correctly.
Cast on 58 sts, using 3mm (US 3) needles and yarn J.
Change to yarns C and P and work 7.5cm (3in) in 2 colour rib as given for back, ending with a RS row.
Next row (inc) (WS) Using yarn P only, P2, (M1p, P18) 3 times, M1p, P2. (62 sts)
Change to 3¾mm (US 5) needles and work in patt from chart between markers for sleeve, beg at row 178 and working down through chart until 134 patt rows have been completed, and AT THE SAME TIME shape sides by inc one st at each end of every 3rd row until there are 138 sts.
Cast (bind) off evenly.

NECKBAND
Press all pieces gently on WS, using a warm iron over a damp cloth and avoiding ribbing.
Join right shoulder seam, using backstitch.
With RS facing, using 3mm (US 3) needles and yarn P, pick up and K32 sts evenly down left front neck, 14 sts across centre front, 32 sts up right front neck and 40 sts across back neck. (118 sts)
Change to yarns C and P and work 5 rows in 2 colour rib as given for back, beg with row 2.
Cast (bind) off evenly in rib, using yarn J.

FINISHING
Use backstitch for all seams on main knitting and an edge to edge st for ribbing.
Join left shoulder seam and neckband.
Sew cast (bound) off edge of sleeve to vertical edge of armhole and sew cast (bound) off edge of armhole to side of sleeve.
Join side and sleeve seams.
Press seams.

The late autumn sun in Cambridge catches the Icon crewneck, its glowing colours resembling stained glass windows.

CONES

Quite often, shop owners plead with me to produce 'something simple' for the less adventurous knitters. My hackles rise as my life has been devoted to challenging knitters to create ever more opulent designs. Yet every once in a while I'm lucky to find a simple design that hints at richness while being a snap to produce. Cones (named after the orangey-red traffic cones used on the highways) is one such design, as it has one-colour-a-row stripes and two-colour fairisle sections. It could be made in many colour combinations using, for instance, a variety of blue tones with pinks, turquoises and yellow-greens.

SIZE AND MEASUREMENTS

One size to fit up to 97cm (38in) bust/chest
Finished measurement at underarm 106cm (42in)
Length from shoulder 54.5cm (21½in)

YARN

Rowan Cotton Glacé, Handknit DK Cotton, and Nice Cotton – all 50g (1¾oz) balls

			Shade no	Amount
A	Glacé	Poppy	741	3 balls
B	Glacé	Watermelon	740	1 ball
C	Glacé	Provence	744	1 ball
D	Glacé	Gentian	743	1 ball
E	Glacé	Dijon	739	1 ball
F	Glacé	Clay	738	1 ball
G	Glacé	Matador	742	1 ball
H	Glacé	Rowan	736	1 ball
J	Glacé	Harebell	732	1 ball
L	DK Cott	Raspberry	240	1 ball
M	Nice	Carnival	432	1 ball
N	Nice	Rio	431	1 ball
P	Nice	Mardi-Gras	436	1 ball
R	Nice	Parade	430	1 ball
S	Nice	Samba	435	1 ball
T	Nice	Adobe	434	1 ball

Note: Yarns are shown on the charts either by their relevant letters or by symbols. Refer to the chart key for symbols.

NEEDLES AND BUTTONS

Pair of 2¾mm (UK no 12) (US 2) needles
Pair of 3¼mm (UK no 10) (US 3) needles
Circular needle 2¾mm (UK no 12) (US 2) 100cm (40in) long
Four buttons

TENSION/GAUGE

25 sts and 32 rows to 10cm (4in) measured over patterned st st using 3¼mm (US 3) needles.

Check your tension (gauge) carefully before beginning and change needle size if necessary.

NOTES

When working the colourwork pattern, use the fairisle method (2 colours a row), carrying yarn not in use loosely across back of work, weaving in every 3 or 4 sts and spreading sts to their correct width to keep them elastic.
Read back and fronts chart from right to left for K (RS odd-numbered) rows and from left to right for P (WS even-numbered) rows.
Read front bands chart from left to right for P (WS odd-numbered) rows and from right to left for K (RS even-numbered) rows.

BACK

Cast on 133 sts, using 2¾mm (US 2) needles and yarn A.
** For hem work 9 rows in st st, beg with a K row, so ending with a K row.
Next row (WS) Knit (to form foldline).**
Change to 3¼mm (US 3) needles and cont in patt from chart (see Notes) for back which is worked entirely in st st, beg with a K row.
Work 90 rows in patt, so ending with a WS row.
Shape armholes
Foll chart throughout, cast (bind) off 6 sts at beg of next 2 rows.
Dec one st at each end of next 8 rows.
Work one row without shaping.
Dec one st at each end of next row and 3 foll alt rows. (97 sts)
Work without shaping until chart row 174 has been completed, so ending with a WS row.
Shape shoulders
Cast (bind) off 5 sts at beg of next 10 rows.
Cast (bind) off rem 47 sts for back neck.

LEFT FRONT

Cast on 67 sts, using 2¾mm (US 2) needles and yarn A.
Work as given for back from ** to **.
Change to 3¼mm (US 3) needles and work 80 rows in patt from chart between markers for left front, so ending with a WS row.
Shape front neck and armhole
Foll chart throughout, dec one st at neck edge on next row and every foll 4th row 23 times in all, and AT THE SAME TIME when front matches back to armhole ending with a WS row, shape armhole as given for back. (25 sts)
Work without shaping until front matches back to shoulder, ending with a WS row.

The Cones waistcoat is the easiest knit in my repertoire, with its two-colour fairisle and simple stripe sections. It is named after highway traffic cones.

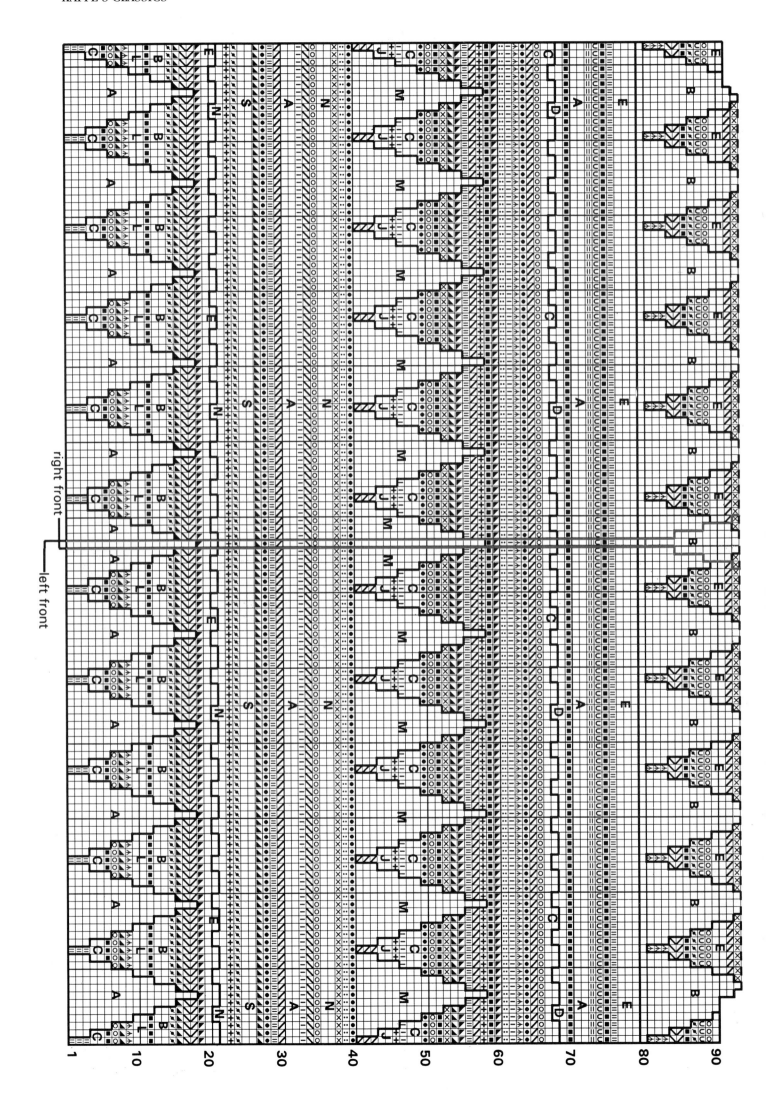

Front band chart

8 st. rep

4 buttonhole row

1

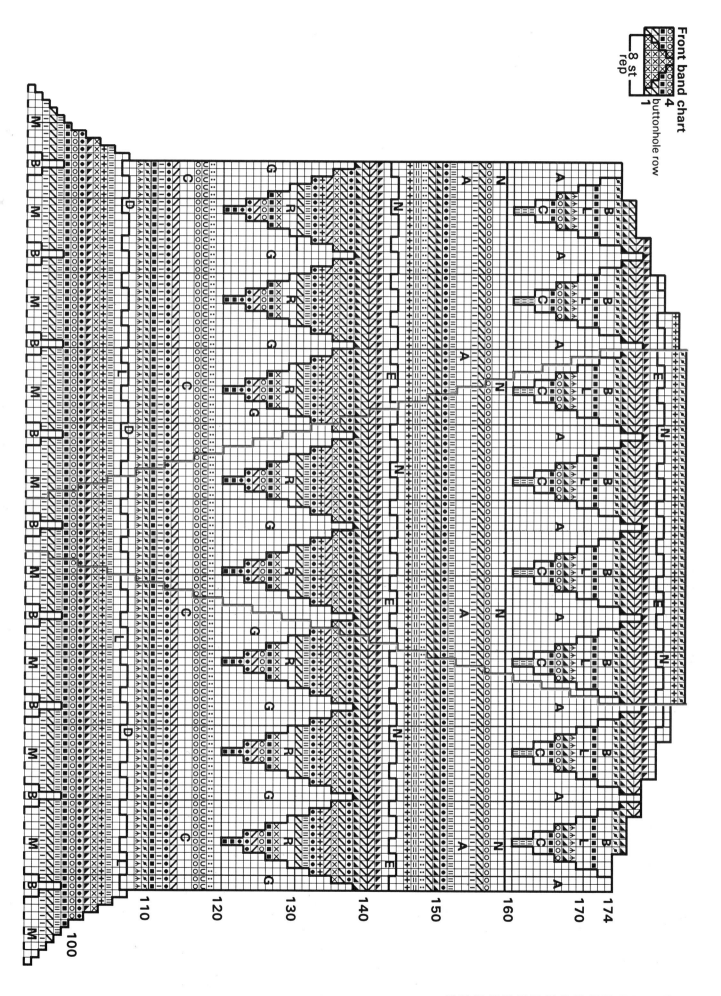

100 110 120 130 140 150 160 170 174

Key
A
B
C
D
E
F
G
H
J
L
M
N
P
R
S
T

135

Shape shoulder
Cast (bind) off 5 sts at beg of next row and 4 foll alt rows.

RIGHT FRONT
Work as given for left front, reversing all shaping and foll chart between markers for right front.

FRONT BANDS (worked in one piece)
Press all pieces gently on WS, using a warm iron over a damp cloth.

Join both shoulder seams, using backstitch.
With RS facing, using 2¾mm (US 2) circular needle and yarn G, beg at foldline on right front and K60 sts evenly up right front edge to beg of neck shaping, 77 sts up right neck edge to shoulder seam, one st at shoulder seam, 45 sts across centre back, one st at shoulder seam, 77 sts down left front neck edge to beg of neck shaping and 60 sts down left front edge to foldline. (321 sts)

Working back and forth in rows (not rounds), work one row in patt from chart for front bands, beg chart row 1 at left-hand side with a purl row and working 8 patt sts 40 times across row, then first st again.

Work buttonholes on rows 2 and 3 for man's *or* woman's version as foll:

Man's version only:
Row 2 (RS) Work 266 sts in patt, (K2tog tbl, take yarn from front to back over top of RH needle, then to front between 2 needles and from front to back again over top of RH needle to make 2 extra sts — called *yarn over twice* or *yo2* —, K2tog, work 12 sts in patt) 3 times, K2tog tbl, yo2, K2tog, K2.

Woman's version only:
Row 2 (RS) K2, (K2tog tbl, yo2 (see Man's version for explanation), K2tog, work 12 sts in patt) 3 times, K2tog tbl, yo2, K2tog, work in patt to end.

Both versions:
Row 3 Work in patt across row, purling into back of each of 2 yo's at buttonhole.
Row 4 Work in patt.
Row 5 Purl, using yarn E.

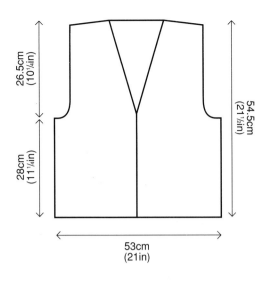

26.5cm (10¼in)
28cm (11¼in)
54.5cm (21½in)
53cm (21in)

Row 6 Purl (to form foldline), using yarn E.
Using yarn A, work 7 rows in st st beg with a P row, and AT THE SAME TIME work buttonholes on rows 3 and 4 to correspond with those already made.
Cast (bind) off very loosely and evenly.

ARMBANDS (both alike)
With RS facing, using 2¾mm (US 2) circular needle and yarn G, pick up and K132 sts evenly around armhole edge.
P one row, using yarn D.
P one row (RS) to form foldline, using yarn D.
Change to yarn A and work 3 rows in st st, beg with a P row.
Cast (bind) off very loosely.

FINISHING
Join side seams and armbands, using backstitch.
Fold hem to WS along foldline and slip stitch loosely in place.
Fold front bands and neckband in half to WS along foldline and slip stitch loosely in place.
Fold armhole facings to WS along foldline and slip stitch loosely in place.
Neatly sew bottom of front bands and facings together.
Sew on buttons to correspond with buttonholes.
Press seams.

JESTER

This is the second design by my assistant Brandon Mably. The inspiration is kilim carpets (a never-ending source of strong ideas). I love the bold primitive use of geometry and rich autumn palette. It works so well against the textures of this old chapel. The outline rusty tone is carried throughout the pattern with diamonds of colours done in intarsia.

The Jester crewneck. Even though you carry the outline colour throughout this design, the lightweight yarns make it a comfortable wear.

SIZE AND MEASUREMENTS

One size to fit up to 102cm (40in) bust/chest
Finished measurement at underarm 117cm (46in)
Length from shoulder 63cm (25in)
Sleeve length 49cm (19½in)

YARN

Rowan Donegal Lambswool Tweed, Lightweight DK, and Kid Silk – all 25g (1oz) hanks/balls

			Shade no	Amount
A	Ltwt DK		8	2 hanks
B	Ltwt DK		104	2 hanks
C	Ltwt DK		77	4 hanks
D	Ltwt DK		5	3 hanks
E	Ltwt DK		53	3 hanks
F	Ltwt DK		11	3 hanks
G	Don Twd	Juniper	482	1 hank
H	Don Twd	Leaf	481	2 hanks
J	Don Twd	Cinnamon	479	8 hanks
L	Don Twd	Sapphire	486	2 hanks
M	Don Twd	Roseberry	480	2 hanks
N	Don Twd	Pickle	483	1 hank
P	Kid Silk	Holly	990	3 balls

Note: Yarns are shown on the chart either by their relevant letters or by symbols. Refer to the chart key for symbols.

NEEDLES

Pair of 3mm (UK no 11) (US 3) needles
Pair of 3¾mm (UK no 9) (US 5) needles
Circular needle 3mm (UK no 11) (US 3) 40cm (16in) long

TENSION/GAUGE

26 sts and 30 rows to 10cm (4in) measured over patterned st st using 3¾mm (US 5) needles.
Check your tension (gauge) carefully before beginning and change needle size if necessary.

NOTES

The pattern is comprised of a series of interlocking diamond motifs. Use separate lengths of yarn (the intarsia method) for each diamond, linking one colour to the next by twisting them around each other where they meet on WS to avoid holes.
Carry the outline colour, yarn J, loosely across the back of the work, weaving in every 3 or 4 sts. Reach chart from right to left for K (RS odd-numbered) rows and from left to right for P (WS even-numbered) rows unless otherwise stated.

BACK AND FRONT (one piece)

Beg at lower back edge, cast on 131 sts, using 3mm (US 3) needles and yarn P.
Work 25 rows in K1, P1 rib in the foll colour sequence:
2 rows P, 3 rows A, 3 rows C, 3 rows B, 3 rows M, 3 rows D, 3 rows E, 3 rows A and 2 rows J.
Next row (inc) (WS) P5, (pick up horizontal loop before next st and purl into back of it — called *make one purlwise or M1p* —, P6) 20 times, M1p, P6. (152 sts)
Change to 3¾mm (US 5) needles and cont in patt from chart (see Notes) for back which is worked entirely in st st, beg with a K row (noting that all the outlines are worked in yarn J).

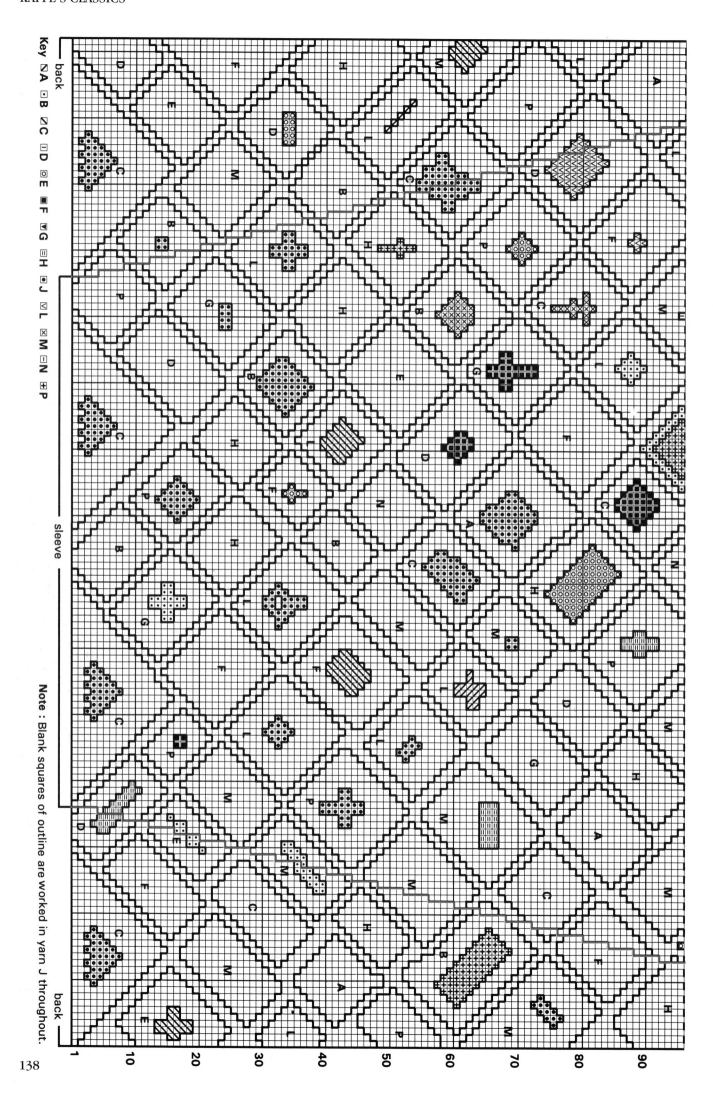

Key ☑A ⊡B ☑C ⊡D ⊙E ◼F ☑G ⊞H ⊡J ☑L ☒M ⊡N ⊞P

back

sleeve

back

Note : Blank squares of outline are worked in yarn J throughout.

shoulder line

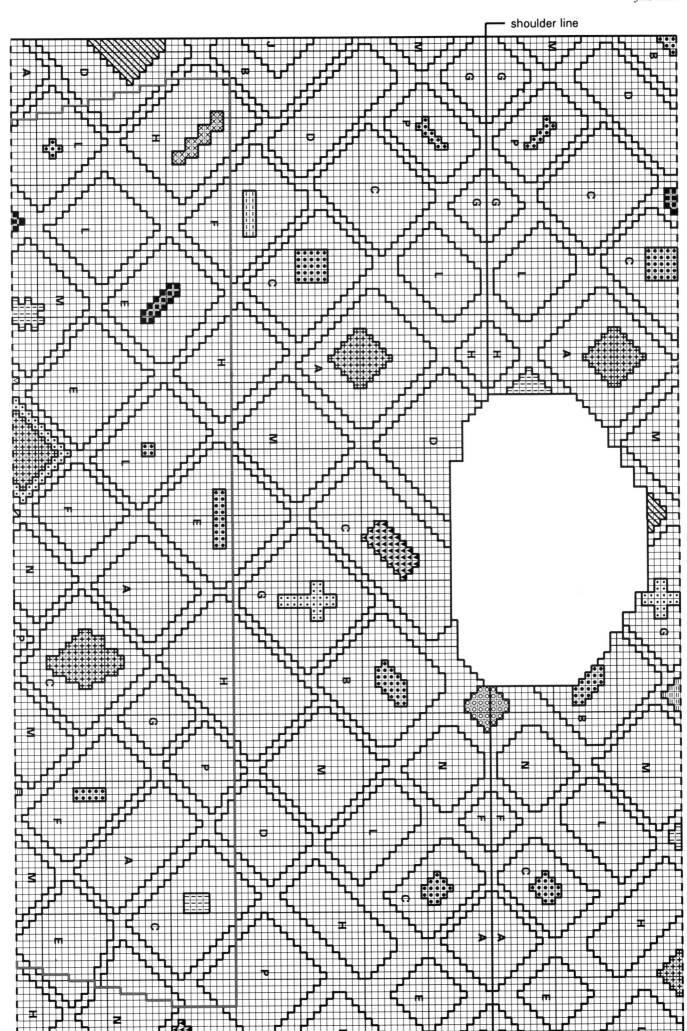

Work 164 rows in patt, so ending with a WS row.

Divide for neck

Chart row 165 (RS) Work 64 sts in patt, then turn and leave rem sts on a st holder.

Work each side of neck separately, foll chart throughout.

Cast (bind) off 6 sts at beg of next row.

Dec one st at neck edge on next 4 rows. (54 sts)

Mark each end of last row (chart row 170) for shoulder line.

Work without shaping until chart row 184 has been completed, so ending with a WS row.

Shape front neck

Inc one st at neck edge on next 5 rows.

Cast on 3 sts at beg of next row and foll 2 alt rows. (68 sts)

Work one row without shaping, so ending with chart row 195.

Leave these sts on a spare needle for right side front neck.

With RS facing, rejoin yarn to rem sts, cast (bind) off centre 24 sts, work in patt to end.

Work one row without shaping, then complete to match first side of neck, reversing all shaping and ending with chart row 195. (68 sts)

Join right and left sides

Chart row 196 (WS) Work in patt across 68 sts of second (left) side, cast on 16 sts, work in patt across 68 sts of first (right) side. (152 sts)

Cont without shaping until chart row 200 has been completed, so ending with a WS row.

Then complete the front by cont in patt from chart for back, beg at row 140 with a K row and working backwards through the rows (cont to read K rows from right to left and P rows from left to right), so ending at row 1 with a P row.

Change to 3mm (US 3) needles and work dec row as foll:

Next row (dec) (RS) Using yarn J, K5, (K2tog, K5) 20 times, K2tog, K5. (131 sts)

Work 25 rows in K1, P1 rib, reversing colour sequence given for back and ending with 3 rows of P instead of 2.

Cast (bind) off evenly in rib, using yarn P.

SLEEVES (both alike)

Cast on 71 sts, using 3mm (US 3) needles and yarn P.

Work 25 rows in K1, P1 rib in colour sequence as given for back.

Next row (inc) (WS) P4, (M1p, rib 8) 8 times, M1p, P3. (80 sts)

Change to 3¾mm (US 5) needles and work 130 rows in patt from chart between markers for sleeve, and AT THE SAME TIME shape sides by inc one st at each end of 5th row and every foll 4th row until there are 140 sts, taking extra sts into patt as they occur.

Cast (bind) off loosely and evenly.

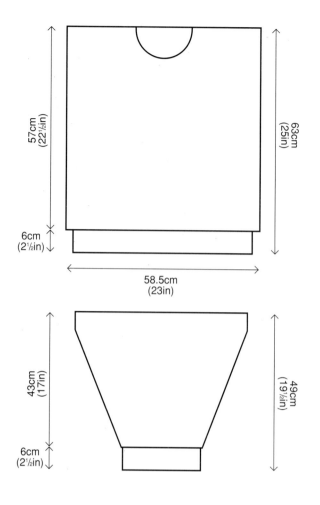

NECKBAND

Press all pieces gently on WS, using a warm iron over a damp cloth and avoiding ribbing.

With RS facing, using 3mm (US 3) circular needle and yarn J, beg at left shoulder line and pick up and K27 sts evenly down left front neck, 16 sts across centre front, 27 sts up right front neck to shoulder line, 10 sts down right back neck, 24 sts across centre back and 10 sts up left back neck. (114 sts)

Work 13 rounds (RS always facing) in K1, P1 rib in the foll colour sequence:

2 rounds J, 3 round B, 3 rounds C, 3 rounds A and 2 rounds P.

Cast (bind) off loosely in rib, using yarn P.

FINISHING

Use backstitch for all seams on main knitting and an edge to edge st for ribbing.

Place markers 27cm (10¾in) down from shoulder line on back and front.

Set in sleeves between markers.

Join side and sleeve seams.

Press seams.

The Jester crewneck in the warm sunlight; Brandon Mably's old kilim colours dance with life.

140

ABBREVIATIONS

alt	alternate
approx	approximately
beg	begin (ning)
cm	centimetre(s)
cont	continu(e)(ing)
dec	decreas(e) (ing)
foll	follow(s) (ing)
g	gramme(s)
in	inch(es)
inc	increas(e) (ing)
K	knit
LH	left hand
m	metre(s)
mm	millimetre(s)
oz	ounce(s)
P	purl
patt(s)	pattern(s)
psso	pass slip stitch over
rem	remain(s) (ing)
rep	repeat(s) (ing)
RH	right hand
RS	right side(s)
sl	slip
st(s)	stitch(es)
st st	stocking (stockinette) stitch
tbl	through back of loop(s)
tog	together
WS	wrong side(s)
yd	yard(s)
yo	yarn over

* Rep instructions after asterisk or between asterisks as many times as instructed.
( ) Rep instructions inside parentheses as many times as instructed.

YARN INFORMATION

It is always best to use the yarn recommended in the knitting pattern instructions. Addresses for Rowan Yarns are given on page 143. If you want to use a substitute yarn, choose a yarn of the same type and weight as the recommended yarn. The descriptions (right) of the various Rowan yarns are meant as a guide to the yarn weight and type (i.e. cotton, mohair, wool, et cetera). Remember that the description of the yarn weight is only a rough guide and you should test a yarn first to see if it will achieve the correct tensions (gauge).

The amount of a substitute yarn needed is determined the number of metres (yards) required rather than by the number of grammes (ounces). If you are unsure when choosing a suitable substitute, ask your yarn shop to assist you.

DESCRIPTIONS OF ROWAN YARNS

Botany – a 4-ply (US fingering) weight yarn
(100% pure new wool)
approx 115m (125yd) per 25g (1 oz) hank

Cabled Mercerized Cotton – a lightweight cotton yarn
(100% cotton)
approx 185m (203yd) per 50g (1¾oz) ball

Chunky Cotton Chenille – a chunky (US bulky) weight yarn
(100% cotton)
approx 140m (153yd) per 100g (3½oz) hank

Chunky Fox Tweed – a chunky (US bulky) weight yarn
(100% pure new wool)
approx 100m (109yd) per 100g (3½oz) hank

Cotton Glacé – a lightweight cotton yarn
(100% cotton)
approx 112m (123 yd) per 50g (1¾oz) ball

Designer DK – a double knitting (US worsted) weight yarn
(100% pure new wool)
approx 115m (125yd) per 50g (1¾oz) ball

Donegal Lambswool Tweed – a 4-ply (US sport) weight yarn
(100% pure new wool)
approx 100m (109yd) per 25g (1oz) hank

Fine Cotton Chenille – a lightweight chenille yarn
(89% cotton/11% polyester)
approx 160m (175yd) per 50g (1¾oz) hank

Fox Tweed DK – a double knitting (US worsted) weight yarn
(100% pure new wool)
approx 110m (120yd) per 50g (1¾oz) hank

Handknit Dk Cotton – a medium weight cotton yarn
(100% cotton)
approx 85m (90yd) per 50g (1¾oz) ball

Kid Silk – a medium weight mohair-silk
(70% kid mohair/30% mulberry silk)
approx 63m (69yd) per 25g (1oz) ball

Lambswool Tweed – a double knitting (US worsted) weight yarn
(100% pure new wool)
approx 125m (137yd) per 50g (1¾oz) ball

Lightweight DK – a lightweight double knitting (US sport) weight yarn
(100% pure new wool)
approx 67m (73yd) per 25g (1oz) hank

Magpie – an Aran weight yarn
(100% pure new wool)
approx 150m (164yd) per 100g (3½oz) hank

Nice Cotton – a lightweight cotton yarn
(100% cotton)
approx 110m (120yd) per 50g (1¾oz) ball

Rowanspun Tweed – a chunky (bulky) weight yarn
(100% pure new wool)
approx 170m (186yd) per 100g (3½oz) hank

Sea Breeze – a lightweight cotton yarn
(100% cotton)
approx 198m (217yd) per 50g (1¾oz) ball

Wool and Cotton – a 4-ply (US sport) weight yarn
(50% superfine botany wool/50% Egyptian cotton)
approx 120m (131yd) per 40g (1½oz) ball

KIT INFORMATION

Kits of the following Kaffe Fassett sweater designs which appear in this book are available from Rowan Yarns:
page 20 KILIM JACKET
page 48 ANCIENT JACKET
page 53 TAPESTRY LEAF JACKET
page 122 SPANISH COMBS CREWNECK

ROWAN YARNS ADDRESSES

Rowan yarns are widely available in yarn shops. For details of stockists and mail order sources of Rowan yarns, please write or contact the distributors listed below.
For advice on how to use a substitute yarn, see pages 142-3.

United Kingdom: Rowan Yarns, Green Lane Mill, Holmfirth, West Yorkshire, England HD7 1RE. Tel: (0484) 681881

USA: Westminster Trading Corporation, 5 Northern Boulevard, Amherst, NH 03031. Tel: (603) 886 5041/5043

Australia: Rowan (Australia), 191 Canterbury Road, Canterbury, Victoria 3126. Tel: (03) 830 1609

Belgium: Hedera, Pleinstraat 68, 3001 Leuven. Tel: (016) 23 21 89

Canada: Estelle Designs & Sales Ltd, Units 65/67, 2220 Midland Avenue, Scarborough, Ontario M1P 3E6. Tel: (416) 298 9922

Denmark: Designer Garn, Vesterbro 33 A, DK-9000 Aalborg. Tel: 98 13 48 24

Finland: Helmi Vuorelma-Oy, Vesijarvenkatu 13, SF-15141 Lahti. TelL (018) 826 831

France: Sidel, Ch Depart. 14C 13840 Rognes. Tel: (33) 42 50 15 06

Germany: Christoph Fritzsch GmbH, Gewerbepark Dogelmuhle, D-6367 Karben 1. Tel: 06039 2071

Holland: Henk & Henrietta Beukers, Dorpsstraat 9, NL-5327 AR. Hurwenen. Tel: 04182 1764

Iceland: Stockurinn, Kjorgardi, Laugavegi 59, ICE-101 Reykjavik. Tel: (01) 18258

Italy: La Compagnia del Cotone, Via Mazzini 44, I-10123 Torino. Tel: (011) 87 83 81

Japan: Diakeito Co Ltd, 2-3-11 Senba-Higashi, Minoh City, Osaka 562. Tel: 0727 27 6604

Mexico: Rebecca Pick Estambresy Tejidos Finos S.A. de C.V., A.V. Michoacan 30-A, Local 3 Esq Av Mexico, Col Hipodromo Condesa 06170, Mexico 11. Tel: (05) 2 64 84 74

New Zealand: John Q Goldingham Ltd, PO Box 45083, Epuni Railway, Lower Hutt. Tel: (04) 5674 085

Norway: Eureka, PO Box 357, N-1401 Ski. Tel: (09) 871 909

Sweden: Wincent, Sveavagen 94, 113 58 Stockholm. Tel (08) 673 70 60

Acknowledgements

Once again it is my pleasure to thank all the helping hands and minds that made this book possible. First of all thanks to my team of knitters Maria, Jules, Charlotte, Francesca, Talitha and the Rowan knitters under their coordinators Kathleen, Kim and Louisa. Thanks to Richard Womersley and all at Ebury, particularly to Polly, Sally and Valerie. Thanks to Tony Boase and especially to Jacky for styling and tasty meals, and to our handsome models. Mostly thanks to Brandon Mably for consistent hard work and good ideas, and to his family for moral support.

Thank you to Kentwell Hall, Long Melford in Suffolk and to Sue Simpson for providing stunning locations; and to Persiflage, Fenwick of Bond Street, Gallery of Antique Textiles, Joanna's Tent, Carlo Manzi Hire, Monsoon and Racing Green for loan of props.

Picture credits
Page 6: (above) Courtesan Wearing a Kimono Decorated with Swimming Carp by Yashima Gakutei, by courtesy of the Trustees of The British Museum.
Page 7: 'Honeysuckle and Sweetpeas' by Winifred Nicholson, City of Aberdeen Art Gallery & Museums Collections; patchwork by courtesy of the Board of Trustees of the Victoria & Albert Museum.
Page 8: Mosaic in Mausoleo di Galla Placidia, Ravenna, Editions Scala; kilim courtesy of Yanni Petsopoulos, Alexandria Press, London.